Wodwo Vergil

Vergil's *Eclogues*

translated by Adam Roberts

Published by Sad Press in Bristol

August 2018

978-0-244-03477-1

Cover artwork by Henri Rousseau

Set in Goudy Old Style

Introduction

The first thing to note is a last thing: the last thing the world needs is another translation of Vergil's *Eclogues*. These ten short-to-middling-length poems stand at the head of a great flowing tradition of pastoral and post-pastoral writing: Spenser's *Shepheardes Calendar*, Shakespeare's *As You Like It*, Goldsmith's *The Deserted Village*, Wordsworth's entire oeuvre, George Eliot's *Adam Bede*, Hardy and hippies, *Akenfield* and Tolkien's Shire, Medbh McGuckian and Ted Hughes, right up to the late modernist ecopoetics of Marcella Durand and Harriet Tarlo, and Green and Environmental aesthetics as a worldwide political movement in our own, uncomfortably-unhomely 21st century. All of that, in one sense, starts here. Critics, interpreters, readers have been all over these poems for millennia. Translators too: they have been rendered into every global tongue, and rendered over and over into the most important global languages. They will continue to be reworked, over and over. Robert Calverley Trevelyan, an early twentieth-century English poet and translator that you have never heard of ('a translator,' the *Encyclopedia Britannica* calls him, 'of a traditionalist sort, and a follower of the lapidary style of Logan Pearsall Smith' if that's any help) prefaced his 1944 version of the *Eclogues* with the following note:

> Virgil's unassailable fame as one of the greatest of poets does not rest upon his *Eclogues*, but upon his *Georgics* and *Aeneid*; yet it has been the fate of these immature experiments to have had a greater

> influence upon European literature than almost any other poems. It was they, rather than their parent Theocritus, that became the fountain-head of the vast stream of Renaissance pastoral writers, Italian, Spanish, French and English. Tasso and Ronsard, Spenser, Sydney and Milton, and the innumerable flock of lesser pastoralists, have all been inspired by and borrowed from them; and their spirit, though not their form, may still be discovered in Adonais and Thyrsis—and also in that pathetic madness of Don Quixote, when he resolved to live the life of an ideal shepherd, 'and entertain himself among the deserts and solitary spaces of that country, where he might freely vent out and give scope unto his amorous passions, by exercising himself in commendable and virtuous pastoral exercises.'

If you care to seek out Trevelyan's own versions of Vergil's poems, you will find them to be accurate, considered and entirely inert. Most English translations are like this, actually. Vergil has become imprisoned by his own inadvertent heritage: decorous, refined, careful, polished, verbally pernickety, syntactically archaic, the filigree white décor on a wedgwood blue plate. Vergilian pastoral became stuck open, as it were; its mechanism jammed, its sunlight, its physical indulgences, its escapism and deliciously mannered artificiality pouring endlessly out and into the channels of literature. The mechanism needs attention, in other words. It would be as absurd as it would be dishonest to suggest that my small-scale undertaking here will make any headway in terms of closing that aperture. Of course it won't. Just speaking practically, people will of course go on translating these poems, and most of those translations will work as part of a well-defined tradition. TS Eliot might even have been right when he claimed that Tradition is a space of disclosure, not enclosure. Nonetheless, what I'm trying to do here is to engage the god Terminus on the side of pastoral.

Let me explain what I mean by that.

Tom Paulin has this to say on the subject of Terminus.

> In Roman mythology, the god Terminus presides over walls and boundaries. He expresses the ancient doctrine that human nature is limited and life irredeemably imperfect. Terminus agrees with Robert Frost in saying 'good fences make good neighbours'; and he also takes a classical view of artistic creation by insisting on formal constraints and closed symmetry. Although Terminus inhabits hedges and drystone walls, he is not a property of pastoral verse, and this is because pastoral writing, like fantasy writing, is a convention which licenses an imaginative freedom from reality. In fantasy literature the result is the ennui of Utopia, a luminous envelope that absorbs the world.

Frost's desperately famous poem opens, of course, with the statement 'something there is that doesn't love a wall'. That something is Nature itself, and if pastoral has any function in the 21st century it must, surely, have to do with the ways the human desire to fence nature around has damaged us more than it has damaged her. Conceivably this is because we have misunderstood the nature of Fantasy itself. Walls are fine, but the Apollonian brickie can't be the only voice singing pastoral. The Dionysian wrecker needs at least to shadow the tune. Or indeed, take lead vocal whilst Apollo songs harmony a third above the melody line. The something that doesn't love a wall, the same thing that through the green fuse drives Dylan's vegetation, needs to be one of the things 'pastoral' is ventriloquising, or we're in serious trouble.

This volume is an exercise in translation that seeks to work against the grain of the original. It's true, of course, that 'work against the grain of' is a polite way of saying 'fuck with,' but I do not propose abandoning *politesse*. Where would that get us? Any given translation does what it does not from sheer perversity but out of a good-faith attempt to engage with the meanings pastoral now deploys. You and I are probably going to agree that 'Nature' has become the single most discursively contested term in modern life, not least because Climate Change is already impinging globally on both nature and culture. You and I are going to agree on that, or you and I are going to have *words*. Now, 'Nature' is not, or not only, or not primarily, a retreat from the stresses or the world. It is not a garden or an Eden or a *locus amoenus*. Nature, increasingly, is that mode of violence that scarifies the borderline of how far Human goes.

So here's Vergil, and here are his *Eclogues*. As far as the original Latin is concerned, the poems inhabit a fairly rarefied, mannered idiom which we have to assume differs from the sort of Latin actually spoken by shepherds, goatherds and suchlike rural commoners—though, of course, we lack any samples of the speech of the latter, which reduces us to assumption and speculation. Still: Robert Coleman, in the standard scholarly edition of the *Eclogues*, says that the language of Vergil's herdsmen, 'though vivid and animated, is on the whole refined, reflecting the urbanity of their creator. They even show, occasionally, some surprisingly pieces of literary erudition'. Since the poems' key character, Tityrus, has been assumed since classical times to be Vergil inserting himself into his own poem, it's not surprising that the Tityran voice is of a more educated sort than the language of actual peasants. An elegant weapon for a more civilized age, as the phrase goes.

Then again, in most of the Vergilian *Eclogues* various sorts of threat and disharmony lurk often not very far below the surface of the sunlit greensward and charming copses of woodland. And disruption is much more the necessity where nature and the representation of nature is concerned. This in turn makes me wonder if the longstanding tradition of translating these poems into a fluent and dignified English idiom might be the wrong way of going about it. What might Vergil's *Eclogues* look like if they were Englished not according to a polished 18th-century nature-poetry vibe, or even a modern celebration-of-Gaia mode, but with more roughness and forcefulness?

There's only one way to find out.

There are antecedents. Christopher Logue's *War Music* version of Homer—he worked on this from the 1970s up to his death in 2011—monkeys-around with the Greek in creative and dislocating ways. Though Logue's *Homer* now has the status of a minor classic, not everyone approved when they were originally published. The best Bernard Knox, reviewing Logue's translation for the *London Review of Books*, could manage was that it 'has its occasional felicities'. More broadly, classicists hated how fast and loose Logue cut with his source material. Respectful nods to, let's say, Ezra Pound's *Homage to Sextus Propertius* might be inserted to suggest that the problem is not the cutting fast-and-loose as such, so much as it is the velocity of the fast and the prodigality of the looseness: 'naggingly satirical', Claude Rawson complained, 'like an *Iliad* rewritten by Thersites'. He added:

> Ironic misapplications of a noble original to modern reality have always been one of the rich resources of the genre, as have secondary suggestions that the revered ancients may after all have been as ignoble as their modern avatars. What grates in Logue's version is the nervous overemphasis. Something is being proved by overkill and the fact diverts attention from the poem, old or new, to the jumpy performing tricks of the poet. The real failure is not in the fidelity of *War Music* to Homer but precisely in its effect as an English poem.

Ouch. I first read *War Music* as a student of English and Classics at Aberdeen University in 1987 and it took the top of my head away. I thought it breathtaking, vital, wonderful. I'm almost afraid to go back to it, now, for fear that I would see only its weaknesses and none of its strengths, and so would confirm to myself that I've turned into a Knox or a Rawson. That would truly be terminal.

At any rate, the translations that follows make no attempt to disguise their Ted Hughesian influences. At the same time they are worked to be as close to the original Latin as possible, such that comparing them with their provenance, or a more literal translation thereof, will clear-up any obscurities. The title triangulates the German and English 'w's with the Latin and English 'v's, but you already noticed that. An essay on pastoral poetry is exiled to the decent obscurity of an appendix.

Eclogue 1

At the origin point of the tradition of writing we call 'pastoral' are two rather different types of poetry. On the one hand are works like Theocritus's *Εἰδύλλια* ['Idylls'] from the 3rd century BC and Vergil's *Eclogues* from the 1st: that is, poems set in an idealised and beautiful natural space, in which shepherds eat good food and pursue lovely maidens and generally live free from hardship and want. In point of fact, even in these earliest works hardship is never very far away; but nonetheless: say 'pastoral' to most people and that's what they'll think of: carefree shepherds in lovely natural surroundings. On the other hand are works like Hesiod's *Ἔργα καὶ Ἡμέραι* ['Works and Days'] from the 7th century BC and Vergil's *Georgics*: which is to say, more practically-minded almanacs or guidebooks on how actually to farm and husband the land. On the one hand poems idealising natural beauty; on the other, gardening handbooks.

The former sorts of poems are sometimes called 'eclogues,' sometimes 'bucolics,' and they tend to articulate a more arcadian, 'fantasy' version of the natural world. Georgics, because they focus on practicalities, have to encompass nature as sometimes hard and resistant to human husbandry, since that is the way the natural world actually is. Digging and ploughing are laborious and difficult in a way that lying in the sunshine blowing a tune on your pan pipe is not.

That said, and just staying with Vergil's *Eclogues* for now, descriptions of countryside pleasures tend to be undercut by broader anxieties. After Caesar's rise, and especially after the wars that followed his assassination in 44 BC, many poorer farmers were booted off their land so that it could be given to retiring soldiers and other friends of the new regime. Indeed, it seems this very thing happened to Vergil. That's the tradition, at any rate: his family farm near Mantua was seized and given to veterans, and he petitioned a family friend, Gaius Asinius Pollio (governor of Cisalpine Gaul, no less), to get it back. Through Pollio he was introduced to the mighty Octavian/Augustus, and through his influence Vergil either got his farm back or else was given money to buy a new farm in Campania. The biographical details are uncertain (indeed, some scholars think it unlikely any of this actually happened). What can't be denied is that Vergil's first and ninth Eclogues are about this very situation: contrasting the happiness of the farmer who retains his land with the misery of the farmer evicted from it.

Eclogue 1

MELIBOEUS
Tityrus, you—recumbent,
brain a blown dandelion
under the knobs and prongs of this beech-trees
flashing the Muse your stiff little flute—but
what about us? Our
country shucks us off, delinquent
ripped from sweetness, fields leathery.
We
vomited out by our own fatherland.
You in a whorl of shade, singing to the undercurrent wooden echo
Littlelove Amaryllis.
Littlelove

TITYRUS
God gave me the binding pentagram of his power.
he'll always taste of god in *my* mouth
I erase the dry bleating of a lamb,
with my knife's blade
frothing the stone altar with blood
only for him;
he is why my cows reel through these fields
he is why I touch my flute with my flat tongue
and gasp it into music.

MELIBOEUS
Not envious, rather
amazed, amazingly amazed.
At every compass point the land is shredding itself into

blood and meat-tasselled bone:
my heart pumps slow and sorry.
Herding my doe goats down the narrow track, and the
one that won't be lead, Tityrus:
twin kids slithered through her maternal noose
wriggled slimy onto bare flints
a hard birthing, and *she's*
the hope of the flock.
Prophesy warned me, oh, over and over,
omen and omen,
when the clouds hauled their burly arms
and swung the sparking axe of lightning
out of the sky to slice the oaks
I should have known then.
But idiocy dragged at my mind.
So, Tityrus, explain him to me, your god.

TITYRUS
God is a city, Meliboeus, clean.
God is Rome.
I was wrong to think Rome like our village,
small mobs of lambs,
puppies are just downsized bitches, right?
Kids model goats? Easy comparing little to big.
That won't do for Rome: giant
cypress looming over low willows,
a prodigy.

MELIBOEUS
So Rome kiss-of-lifed you?

TITYRUS
Finally, Freedom
telescoped my incompetence, just
as my beard was whitening.
Freedom surveilled me for eons, I reckon,
but lurked, held back
until I finally got together with Amaryllis,
after Galatea left.
When Galatea squatted on my chest
like the nightmare, I had no hope
she my obsession
freedom was nothing to me then, my money was nothing,
only she mattered, lust and conscience,
whimpering together under the covers,
selling my flock
I couldn't shoo them quickly enough out of their stalls
selling my smoothest cheeses in the town
none of it mattered
my hands clutching zero pounds no shillings no pence.

MELIBOEUS
I used to wonder why Amaryllis
wailed *god god* so often,
and whose were the pending apples
clogging the trees.
Tityrus had absconded, it seemed.
Yours was the name the pine trees creaked,
You, Tityrus,
Fountains and orchards hissed you.

TITYRUS
What option did I have? None.
Slavery would not ungrip me.

Regular gods were indifferent.
Until, Meliboeus: until the young one came.
We jib-up altar-fires
twice six times a year, burning for that young one
a grasping ungrasping claw of flame,
bundles of smoke unloaded into the sky,
here:
he was the first to answer me, with
parcel food to the cows, lads, upraise the bullocks.

MELIBOEUS
You lucky old bastard, keeping your own land,
wide as a park, though cluttered with bare stones
and although bogs cram sliming rushes
down the throat of your meadows. Still!
At least you won't make your breeding ewes
ill
by feeding them foreign weeds, yours won't
catch bluetongue or river fever from foreign herds.
Lucky old bastard. Here, by this stream
as familiar to you as your own morning piss,
under hot sun, in refrigerated shade;
here
you always
local, horizoned by that hedge,
Hybla bees with their probosci
eyeballs-deep in willow blossom
swarm a hum the sound of friction; and
wood pigeons swaddling you with cooing
and doves whining from those skyscraper elms.

TITYRUS

Yeah *I'll* leave, when stags graze on the high sky
eating ether, and fish flee the ocean
and stripping naked on the beach;
I'll leave, but only when Parthians swig
water from the Arar, and Germans fill their
beer-bellies at the fucking Tigris. Not before.

MELIBOEUS

We're off, though. Shards of mankind
some of us to dry Africa
mauve-dry dust and thirsty,
some to Scythia, wherever that is,
some to where the cold river Oaxes
hurtles through Crete,
some even so far as Britain.
Say I return, in a millennium or so,
see a few pegs of blonde corn

standing amongst bobbling weeds
and think: that used to be my kingdom.
Godless squaddies goosestepping
over my ploughlines
Soldier farmers
barbarians now
war
has fractured the civilian world.
We worked this rebarbative land
for them, not for ourselves.
A diagonal cut to graft your pears, Meliboeus,
a straight row to plant your vines.

Off we go, goats, off we go now
this isn't us any more
this isn't me, in a swoon of meadowland
staring at the bright sky,
this isn't me singing
this isn't you, goats, browsing toothily
on willowleaves and alfalfa.

TITYRUS
It was here, it was one single night,
plucked from the wreck,
leaves green as seaglass
pearl-red apples
chestnuts crumbling in the mouth and
pressed cheeses.
Glooms of smoke creep from the chimneys, over there,
the mountains drum down shadows
darkening around us.

Eclogue 2

Vergil's second eclogue, though numbered '2,' may well have been the first written. It is pretty closely based on two of Theocritus's *Idylls*—his third, in which a neglected lover bemoans his condition, and his eleventh, in which the Cyclops Polyphemus is hopelessly in love with the sea-nymph Galatea, and finds solace for his pain in singing. Vergil's shepherd's name, 'Corydon,' means songbird: (from the Greek κόρυδος, 'lark'). It's a name that comes from Theocritus's fourth Idyll, then (obviously) by Vergil, and then a few decades later by Titus Calpurnius in his *Eclogues*, such that pretty soon it became the stock name for a shepherd, and later Classical and English Renaissance pastoral is crowded with Corydons. The name Alexis is from Ἄλεξις (which means 'helper, defender') and is related to the heroic warrior name Alexander; so I like to think that the Alexis of this poem is pretty beefy. Hard to be sure, of course.

Eclogue 2

Beauty slammed the shepherd Corydon hard
the beauty of Alexis
his master's pet
        love burning in the lungs of Cory's soul.
To numb his pain
here he comes, moping through the tree-maze
threading the entrails of woodland
beeches that hoard shade in their summits

and he sings his inanity to the hills:

"Virulent Alexis,
my birdsong songs mean nothing to you.
Your lack of pity is an incomprehensible
hieroglyph,
you will inevitably laboriously
                eventually kill me.
Even the hot cows, fierce with
joyful breath, even they
suck relief from the webs of shade;
verdigris lizards
vanish down the plughole of a
thistle-textured thornhedge. Thestylis
grinds a sludge from savoury herbs
        oily garlic, thyme,
stiff pestle driving into the yearning mortar
over and over, reapers sweating, scorched,
standing erect against the blindness of sunlight.

Not me.

I bloodhound *your* traces
through wildernesses of vegetation
copses huddled against the sun's
silent first-day-of-the-Somme
bombardment of heat
and only the cicadas are singing
their withered song
only the cicadas only
and me.

Maybe I should have swallowed
the petulant sourness of that girl Amaryllis,
or maybe gone after Menalcas
though his skin is dark as soil
and yours is white like
purity itself
ice-cumbered, cloudlessly
cloud-blank.
But boy, you can't rely forever on the
come-fuck-me bloom of your skin.
It will happen to you, the same thing that
happens to the pale privet and its
grape-clusters of white flowers:
slashed, bladed and rooted out.
The mauve hyacinths too:
wrecked, and left to rot.

You disrespect me, Alexis. You don't know me at all.
You don't know how rich in cows,
how much the milk tycoon I am.
I own no fewer than one thousand lambs
distributed all over the Sicilian hills.
Abundance of milk, it gushes for me
summer and winter, sweet white fluid
in my mouth and spilling over my mouth.
    I model my singing on Amphion, from Dirce,
    and how he would croon the herds home
    over fields in Aracynthus, in Greece.

Handsome too,
                    though I say so myself,
I mirror-admire myself,
why not?
when the winds go limp, and the waters
settle into lithe stillness
the curve of shore becomes my boudoir
the sea itself my who-is-the-fairest-of-them-all
hushing, *it's me, it's me.*
Daphnis thinks so too.
Reflected beauty is truth. Image makes magic.

Oh! imagine if you consented to dwell where I dwell
a small cottage in the open fields,
toad-shaped under thatch,
squatting under the hill
home, and we would hunt together
shoot arrows to prick down deer,
grasp the green osier-wand to whip

the rocking rumps of our straggling flock!
You and me, love, you and me,
        singing together
songs from the forestlands
more tuneful than Pan himself,
prime Pan, godfather of music
maker of musical instruments, a god and
a lover of sheep, and shepherds of sheep.

You would not regret
fitting the stalk of the flute's
erect length into your mouth,
        to chafe your lip.
Do it like Amyntas used to.
Seven tubes unequally long
waxed together make up my pipe.
Damoetas gave it to me, and that made
Amyntas jealous, the idiot.
It's yours. Take it!
And more than that: a duo of roe-goats
jetsam of a dangerous valley
hides leoparded with white spots
so young they syphon
a whole udderful of milk every day.
I'm keeping them for you.
Thestylis begs me for them, on her knees,
head at crotch-height,
kneel all she likes, they're yours,
they're my gift to the gem light in your eyes.

Come over here, you beauty: you get
gifts of heaped nymph lilies.
Naiad, so in love, in love with you,
gashes violet petals from their stems, shreds
poppy heads, rust-scarlet, unseams
narcissus and sugar-smelling fennel flower;
winds them into a rope
with sepia cassia and other sweet herbs,
tangles in fragile hyacinth
and citrine marigolds.
My own fingers will fumble at
quinces, skin fuzzed with the cilia of pale down,
        and chestnuts.
Amaryllis always loved those.
Plums, waxen globules, maroon
as a glans. I gather that fruit too.
Some laurels—yes, you, laurels
I'm taking you down from your branch, chuckling to myself
and your friend, myrtle,
both sweet savourable odours.

Oh what a fucking peasant you are, Corydon.
Like Alexis cares for gifts!
Like that would even seduce, I don't know,
Iollas, even.
Fuck my life.
Seriously.
What was I thinking? The south wind
slips past me and mugs my flowers,
and while I was moping after that boy, wild boar
have pigged their way into my clear wells of water.

I'm demented. Who am I even running from?
Gods have taken trees as walls and roof
Dardan Paris too.
Pallas fitted together the jigsaw pieces
into full-sized cities
tiled and tessellated and undulating with bright roofs
the way only a goddess can
so she can live there.
Forest is my passion.
The lioness with the psycho-eyes pursues the wolf,
a thousand yard stare
it's a distance she covers in seconds;
the wolf runs down she-goat, even the she-goat
gets to tear the innards from
the flowering broom bushes,
and Corydon
and Alexis,
each keelhauled by their own longing.
Here comes the ox, home
with plough up-tilted like a heiling arm.
Tumescent shadows grow and harden
to twice their length
as the sun ducks and covers, arms over its head,
chin on its knees, a bundle of
night terrors.

This love has simmered and scorched my heart
blackened it, blistered me,
done everything but numb me.
I can't stop feeling it
Ah! Corydon, Corydon, searing.
You haven't pruned your dangling vine
slopping its dreadlock off the leaf-swarming elm;
weave pliant wicker together? Scorned
scorned.
Go looking for a new Alexis."

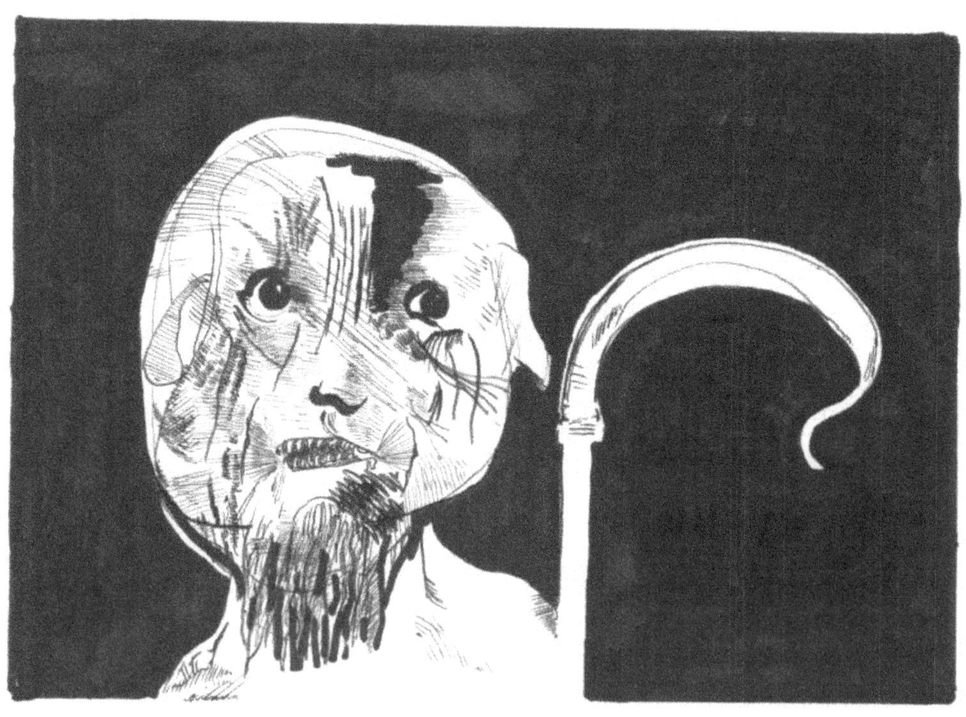

Eclogue 3

It's not easy to know what to do, translation-wise, with how often Vergil's eclogues are about singing contests between shepherds. Rural singing contests are not something that possess any contemporary purchase or meaning (I did, briefly, think in terms of rap battles, but the world breathed a collective sigh of relief as this particular white middle-aged man stepped away from that idea). It is a ticklish, though not uninteresting, question: how might we best rework such a thing in modern English cultural and linguistic idiom? The latter factor is, in a way, harder: 'dancing about architecture,' as they say. But the former may be more tractable. Popular songs have been one of the unmistakeable triumphs of late 20th-century culture, and provide a shared idiom for hundreds of millions of people. It ought to be possible to at least gesture towards that in a translation.

One incidental detail of this eclogue is the sideswipe at 'Maevius and Bavius', real poets favoured, it seems, by Roman official power in the 1st century BC, despite the fact that they were, it seems, very bad. Since none of their verse has survived, we have to take Vergil's word for their badness; but everybody seems to have been happy to do exactly that (Cambridge classicist John Henderson calls them 'triumviral poetry's Beavis and Butthead').

Me, I feel a twinge of pity for them, condemned for all eternity on no evidence whatsoever. Conceivably they were better than posterity can allow itself to conceive. As poetry 'she loves you, yeah, yeah' is very far from good; yet nonetheless 'She Loves You' is a great pop song; and in our post Dylan-the-Nobel-Laureate world that, surely, has to count for something.

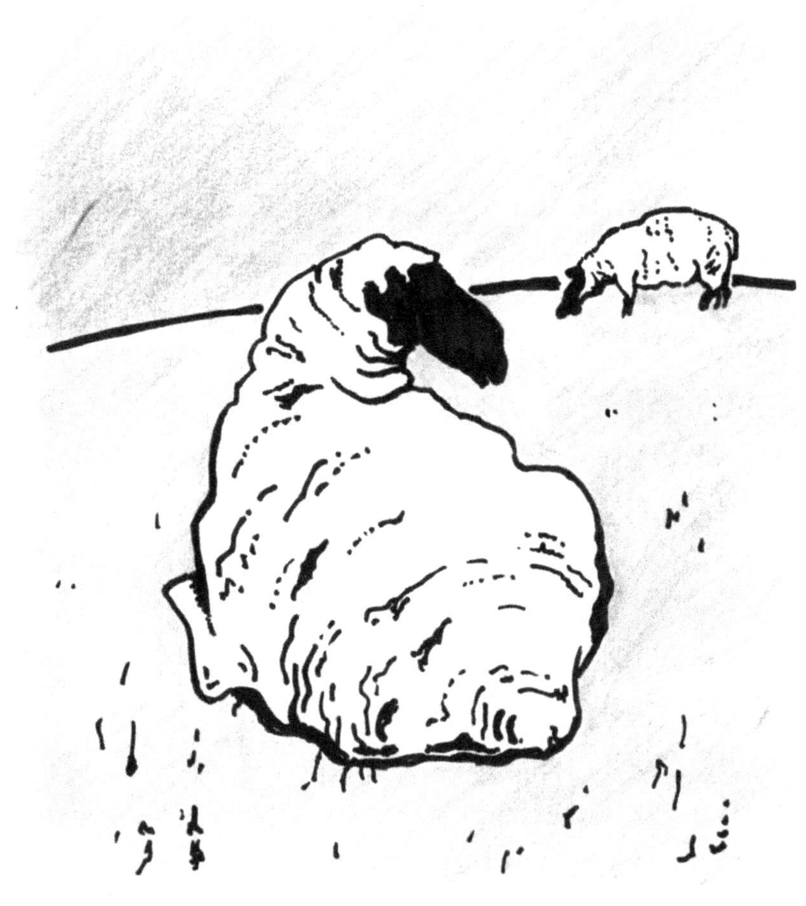

Eclogue 3

MENALCAS
So, these sheep, eh Damoetas?
Meliboeus', are they?

DAMOETAS
Mate, not his. Aegon's, isn't it.
And this is me, minding them.
Aegon trusts me.

MENALCAS
Oho, that's this lot fucked, then.
Off on a date, is he?
And while your boss's hands are on Neara's tits
like a kid with playdoh
you'll be all over these suede udders
groping out six times the usual flow of milk,
stealing sustenance from the lambkins' little mouths
glutting yourself, selling the surplus, leaving
ewes as giddy-weak
as marathon-runners crossing the line,
legs all rope.
Naughty.

DAMOETAS
Fuck off.
You think I don't know
who you've been doing? And with what fervour?
Do me a favour.

MENALCAS
Careful now. You ever seen me use a knife?

DAMOETAS
Oh, so scared, isn't it?
Veritably quaking.
Check out these trees, yeah?
Treat yourself to a longer look.
I like to think of these old-boy beeches as
witnesses. They stand, they surveil.
Perfect recall, isn't it?
They watched when you knacked that bow across your knee
stunned it to splinters, threw the pieces in the sedge.
The bow-and-arrow was given to young Damon,
and you, browned-off for not getting it.
Moody Menalcas, you sulky fucker.

MENALCAS
Oho. You didn't steal Damon's goat, then?
My fucking mistake. My miscuntderstanding.
That wasn't you, whilst the boy's dog, Lycisca,
kept hammering away at the anvil of his barking
over and over,
as if barking was the only idea in his head?
Nah, saw you, mate. Called to Tityrus, didn't I,
and you ducked behind the fucking hedgerow.

DAMOETAS
He owed me that goat, isn't it.
Won it fair and square,
squire.

MENALCAS
Right: You sang a whole fucking cantata
and he wheezed old king cole,
so you won, right?
Thing is, you can no more carry a tune than
clouds can hold onto the weight of their own hard rain.
Your singing is piss through a colander.
You sound like a worn-down brake-pad.
I've shat turds with a better top end
no word of a fucking lie.

DAMOETAS
Care to put your money where your
hairy sack-shaped mouth is?
I'll bet you this heifer; a twice-a-day milker.

MENALCAS
Seriously, though, mate:
if I bet one of these sheep, my Dad
will fucking kill me, and my stepmother
will rip off my balls with nails
lacquered black like ten raven beaks.
So fuck that for a game of shepherds.
No, mate
no
I bet you: cups, that's it.
Alcimedon centred them on his centrifuge
spun and scraped the wood away
like candyfloss in reverse,
until they were shapely as hourglasses. Then
he worked vines into the sides with his burin
ivy berries like a cluster of
sweet little hemorrhoids

and standing under them two men
Conon, one, and
I forget the name of the other geezer.
Holding a wand, though, so maybe Gandalf.

DAMOETAS
Nah, babe, I already got two Alcimedon cups, isn't it,
and mine have *handles*, you loser.
Mine have Orpheus on them, in a tangle
of forest matrix as it locks about him, in love with him.
Hardly worth a cow, though, is it? Some cups?

MENALCAS
Whatever. Bet's on, fucker.
Your cum's thin as piss and mine's fucking gold-top.
All we need's a judge, impartial-like.
And, bingo, here comes Palaemon. He'll do.
For a singing comp he'll doo-be-doo-be-doo.

DAMOETAS
Bring it.

PALAEMON
Gents, let's park our derrieres
on this dollar-green grass, right here.
Pastures and trees and all that, burgeoning
all around us
my friends, truly burgeoning.
The trees stand high as a ship's mast: and
foliage aye came gliding by as green as
aim-air-auld.
Hi-de-hi. Damoetas, you go first, sir.
Then you, Menalcas.

Damoetas
"You'd think that people woulda
had enough of silly Jove-songs
I asked the Muse now and she said
it isn't so
oh no."

Menalcas
"Phoebus loves me
yeah, yeah yeah
Phoe loves me
yeah yeah yeah
and with hyacinths
she gives me what I need."

Damoetas
"Gay Galatea
Gay Galatea
Gay Galatea
Chucks me an apple,
Then runs to the willows
Ooh I gotta see her
I gotta see her
Galatea."

Menalcas
"I don't got to beg her
Amyntas comes down;
my dogs don't bark
my dogs don't bark
when she comes round."

DAMOETAS
"I got my eyes on a
gift for my love
I got my eyes on a
gift for my love
in the skies is my
gift for my love
where pigeons fly
is my gift for my love
gift for my love."

MENALCAS
"Ten gold apples
I gave to that boy.
Ten gold apples
I gave to that boy.
And if he'll just kiss me
I'll give him ten ones more
and he'll have
Twenty gold apples
lying on his floor."

DAMOETAS
"Every little breeze seems to whisper
Galatea
whispea
Galatea
Birds in the trees seem to twitter
Galatea
twittea
Galatea."

MENALCAS
"It breaks my heart to see you go
Iollas
You say farewell I'm filled with woe
Iollas
Oh Iollas"

DAMOETAS
"She don't have to be beautiful
To be his girl
She just use her country-breeding,
To rock his world.
She don't have to be rich
For Pollio
She don't got to own cows
To make him go
Oh Pie-ri-an maids
he is com-pat-i-ble with–"

Menalcas
Alright alright. Fucking hell, already.
Let me just clear my throat.

"Pollio
Pollio
baby
You know I'm in need of you?
Pollio
Pollio
baby
Don't you believe it's true?"

DAMOETAS
You're just embarrassing yourself.
Stand back, I'm going to blast this next one, go
full Adele in the dale:

"And with the Polliooo
When things crumble
We will stand tall-
all-he-all
face it altogether;
stay with Pollio
when things crumble
we will stand tall-all-all
Face it all
together
with Pollio."

MENALCAS
You'll do yourself a mischief
hernia or there-nia. Settle down, my boy.

"I get no kick from sham Bavius,
His rubbish verse doesn't thrill me at all
But baby, Maevius's true:
That I get a goat
Out of you."

DAMOETAS
"My Apollo
Oh mist rolling in from the sea
You must know
the whole breadth of heaven
sees you
Apollo."

MENALCAS
"You make me dizzy
Miss Phyllis,
kings are on the line;
you make me dizzy
Miss Phyllis
they all think you're so fine;
come on Miss Phyllis
come and love me all the time."

PALAEMON
Enough!
Fuck me.
Bacchus on a badger that was bad.
Each as atrocious as at-nother.
You've worked yourselves into
a right two-and-eight.
Boys, boys, shut off
your fucking sluices,
for the fields have drunk their fill.

Eclogue 4

The fourth eclogue has a good claim to being the single most famous short poem ever written, certainly the most famous artefact of non-epic Classical Latin literature. This is because its hazily-framed promise that a saviour baby was about to be born (almost certainly designed to be non-specific enough that various political big beasts of the day, such as Pollio or Octavian, might read and be flattered into thinking their sprog was the foretold saviour) connected powerfully with whole generations of later medieval and Renaissance Christian readers. They decided that this poem, despite having been written four decades *before* the birth of Christ, was nonetheless somehow magically *about* the birth of Christ. This sense of Vergil as a virtuous pagan who somehow poetically intuited Christ's salvation has had an incalculable impact upon the way his verse has been read and understood. For a long time he was seen as white wizard and prophet as much as a poet; the 'Sortes Vergilanae' are only one manifestation of this mode of popularity: open your copy of the *Aeneid* at random, lay your finger on a Latin hexameter, that line will tell your fortune, or answer whichever question you have asked. Try it!

In 'Denial, Anger, Acceptance' (1999), the third episode of *The Sopranos*' first season, James Gandolfini's Tony runs into difficulties collecting a debt from a Hasidic Jew called Shlomo Teittleman. Tony has his men threaten and beat Shlomo, but to no avail. Even threatening him with death doesn't shift Shlomo's resolve. "You ever heard of Masada?" he asks Tony, from the floor. "For two years, 900 Jews held their own against

15,000 Roman soldiers. They chose death before enslavement. And the Romans? Where are they now?" In perhaps my favourite moment from that whole series, Gandolfini looks down on him and replies: "You're looking at em." Sicilian Muse, indeed.

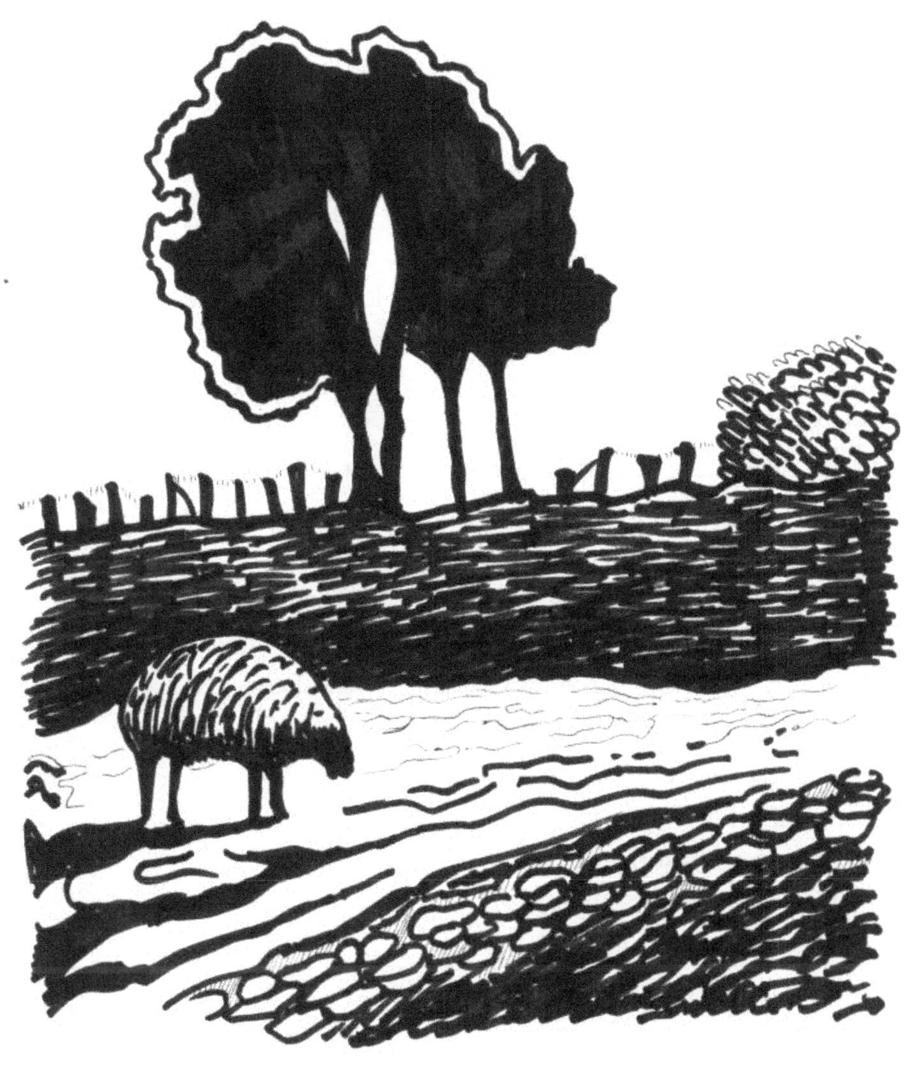

Eclogue 4

Mafia Muses of Sicily, time to raise the tone.
We don't all cream our pants
at orchards or stunted salt cedar bushes. *Capisce?*
If we got to talk about woods,
let em be woods worthy of a *capo di tutti capi*.

It's the last gasp of that witch from Cumae
round it comes again, as
everything always swings round again:
ten decades per century, stacked like crates
piled up to millennia, over, again.
Some sweet teenage girl, never been kissed, steps in
and she's equal measure scared and proud.
And here's the old guy, Saturn Barbabianca: he's in charge now.
He's back, yeah. You'd better fucken believe it.
Whole new crew, youngbloods, straight off the boat
the ferry down from high heaven
strutting.
All for this newborn *bambino*, this kid, come
to break through the iron logic of the world
remake it, through the eye, through the mouth.
Golden, he is: golden; and all his crew are
dorato too. Lucina does the honors.
Apollo is now Boss.
You'd better do what he says.

Credit where it's due:
you deserve this praise, Pollio.
You're the Don, you oversaw this regime change

shining months driving fast on.
You bring *not-guilty* and *no-charge-to-answer*
to all of us, every one:
thanks to you *mio amico* it's no more looking over our shoulders,
nothing more to fear from the wide world.
You're capo when this kid comes in,
and that means *none* of us get whacked
none of us ever again.
We're all made, and for ever.

Every day now pay-day. All doors and windows
open. Safes cracked wide like
church doors at a wedding.
Gardens, sure: cute, if you like that kind of thing.
Ivy in green ribbons draped all over
foxgloves and acanthus
and that plant they call elephant ears.
Nice.
Thirsty? Hey: all you can drink!
on the house buddy!
Hungry? Fill your boots!
And as for our rivals, the Leones?
We don't got to worry about them no more.
And that just leaves the rat, that fucker,
that *serpente*
oh, we'll spring clean that snake,
you can forget about him;
place of his poisonous reek
we'll have all the perfumes of fucken Araby, trust me, trust me.

We gotta respect who came before, fathers
and their fathers,
and theirs, sure:
they had balls. No question.
Walked the fields, drank good *vino*,
made good trades. No question.
Shipped stuff in, sold at good profit,
paid their tributes.
I'm not saying all that has been flushed away, all gone;
some assholes will remain to remind us
of how our fathers went to war, or moved
containers over the gray shapes of the sea.
It all comes round again,
Achilles gotta go to war with Troy again,
over and over.

Until, that is—until our kid exits puberty,
and becomes *uomo*,
and he'll have balls of steel.
Then all our hard work will be over
fucken over.
Easy times ahead, then:
think of it like Dorothy, when everything blooms
from black-and-white into *arcobaleno* technicolour;
sheep in the fields no longer fucken white
but rainbow psychedelic coloured wool,
shifting from purple to yellow like *rosso d'uovo*
to blood-red.
Woh.
Madre di Dio this is some strong shit.
Deep breath out.

Look:
Destiny don't back down, no matter how
you square up to her. It's happening, she says:
it slides on like something
really smoothly lubricated.
And all her crew call out in one voice
Fucken A, they sing.
Fucken A.

Time to get what's coming. The deadline is almost here.
This thing of ours.
You ever look at the world, like,
really look at it?
It's a great dome, some real
supernatural architecture, roof so smooth
and high
you can't even touch it in a jet, not even
those invisible ones the Air Force fly
made of black ceramic
or some shit like that, going faster than music
faster than light can catch up with
not even then. And the air is thin up there,
so, and, *that's* why I keep coughing, *capisce*?
Cold like frost lining the inside of the lungs.
And from so high, looking down
the sea is texture like an untuned TV channel
bright and gray and white and impossibly far deep.
This bambino, though:
he'll step over this whole vault, like
stepping over the corpse of a rival,

bleeding on the sidewalk, and you got somewhere you need to be.
This whole dome and everything inside it
will kiss his ass
and sing his fucken praises. Believe me.

We gotta go, pay our respects to his mother.
Birthing a baby, that's hard work: shitting
a bowling ball, they say.
You gotta get me some more of this shit.
This shit is the proper shit, no question,
forget about it. Little bambino
smiles around him. Think of the deals he'll do
the girls he'll bang. Let's go.

Eclogue 5

Another singing-contest eclogue, this, although less belligerent than some of the others. Menalcas and Mopsus each singing elegies for the death of the beautiful shepherd Daphnis. The deal with this young man was that he was the supposed inventor of pastoral poetry itself: the son of Hermes and a nymph, his mother exposed him under a laurel tree, where some shepherds found him, naming him after the tree (δάφνη, daphne, 'bay laurel'). So this poem is doing more than lamenting one individual; it is a pastoral poet writing two pastoral poets in order for them to elegise pastoral poetry itself. It is hardly surprising that this textual switchback provoked commentators from earliest times into gestures designed to straighten it out: 4th-century grammarian Servius detailed a reading whereby Daphnis was Julius Caesar, and this eclogue an allegory for Vergil and another Roman grieving over Caesar's assassination. My own temperament happens to prefers metatextual knottiness to the faux-solutions of allegory, a mode I cordially dislike. That may just be me.

Eclogue 5

Menalcas said: the core of it, now, is
we're both good men, well met.
Well met. Here
between the giant green quiffs of these elms
with hazels growing in the gaps, in we go.

Mopsus said: you, older than me, should
lead the way. Through weed-coloured shadows
towards this cave and its bead curtain of vines
I follow.

Menalcas said: we're both good poets, well met.
Well met.
Who's better, in all this hilly country?
Maybe only Amyntas.

And Mopsus concurred.

Menalcas said: you start then. Subject: Phyllis,
her beauty. Or: Alcon. Or: Codrus's jollies.
Don't fret about sheep. Tityrus'll tend the sheep.

Mopsus said: I could, I don't know, maybe,
how about, how about maybe my Daphnis one?
I scritched it into the bark of a green beech,
words and stave and tadpole notes threaded on the lines.
Is it as good as Amyntas though? I don't know.

Menalcas said: the way a willow looks
like a blurred photo of itself,
lens twitched up at just the wrong time?
That's him. He's the copy.
You're the electroplated leaves of an olive
shining bosky silver in the sunlight.

So Mopsus said: "Daphnis' life cut off, as the sabre slides on through where the bottle-neck bulges to its cork-brained head, and snap, gushings of foaming grief, and it fizzes in your gut, and the Nymphs' faces a mess of tears and snot, hazels in their despair throwing bush-branches wide like wings, the very rivers bereaved, his mother grappling with the corpse like a drunken wrestler, shouting *gods: cruel* and *stars: cruel* and one African lion, mouth a gluey gash, puts a voice to its roaring grief, and tigers too, tigers, tigers, harnessed like shire horses, and Bacchus, drinking to forget, reeling around the fountain, and the vine cords itself about trees like veins and arteries in blue and red, and after the Fates carried your body off, shoulder high, your arms were all gibbon-floppy, a life-sized manikin, dead. Pales has debouched from our fields, and even Apollo has gone, and all the stalks of barley have shot off on their million miniature rockets into orbit and the furrows a centre parting to weeds lank as unwashed hair, and the bully thistles have flourished their razors at the narcissi and glassed the soft violets, in the face no less, and taken over the whole row, and the sky has emptied its binbag of old leaves all over the ground and a solar eclipse puts a shadow filter on the world's lens, and on the gravestone it says Daphnis/[INSERT DATES HERE]/Lived in the woods/Famed beyond them/*Drop Dead Gorgeous*."

Menalcas said: your words unknot the world.
They strop the leather band of my heart like a razor.
They are their own body.
They are the trickling echo of water in the Zen garden.
They unbreak horses and manumit housepet cats and dogs.
And now it's my turn.

Mopsus said: the prospect of you singing is a gift as big as the sun
It is as close as the moon.
It is an aircraft sliding like a rice grain
over the blue ceramic of high sky
drawing a bridal train contrail behind it.
It's the shivery pulse in my jugular.
It is all Stimichon promised, years ago.

So Menalcas said: "Daphnis approaching the Door Itself, squinting in the light, presses the brass nubbin, and a bell spills metallic vibration into the depths of the house, and his feet are standing on a doormat of clouds and stars, and subaerially the woods and all the countryside dance beneath him, dance, dance like nobody's looking. Pan is wearing both tehmat and chagi and he dances Bhangra, the shepherds shug, the Dryad girls lindy hop, a wolf buries his tilted face in the wool of a sheep and weeps real tears of real remorse for all the evil he previously did to sheepkind as the ghost of Daphnis stand right there and says *peace, man, peace*, mountains with hippy beards of woodland do the stomp, and groves of trees are struck like cymbals, *god is alive and he is Menalcas* so be kind to one another all you folk and don't do evil, and *hwaet*!s this? *Four* altars!—two, see, for you, Daphnis; two, see, for you Phoebus. That's why I say we fill two cups with milk so fresh it foams like white beer. I say two osaka Japanese porcelain bowls topped up with olive oil as thick as diesel, I say: nibbles, of course, and of course wine—winter vintage, cooled, bubbles at the brim like a curving line of perfectly arranged couscous grains. This bottle is a little dusty, but the label says Chian, and that says it all. Damoetas and Lyctian Aegon are going to sing for me, and Alphesiboeus will hoof the beat with his dancing feet. It's a wake, for the best of guys, which means there's a liturgy we have to follow now: give our word of honour to the Nymphs, and purify our fields with monoammonium phosphate and various kinds of potassium sulfate. From behind that boar looks like Cousin It. From above those fish look shavings of pure silver. From where we're sitting the bees look like dust caught in a tiny whirl of updrifting breeze. From what I can hear the cicadas are laughing. Here's a glass to you, Daphnis, here's mud in your eye, here's a health to Bacchus and Ceres, and year after year."

Mopsus said: what would be an acceptable gift?
To reward such a song, I mean?
It was sweeter than the natural sibilance of the south wind.
It would no more quit
than the randy ocean will quit banging the shoreline.
It is as lovely as zigzag streams,
inset by God the Goldsmith into the mountainside.

Menalcas said: gifts, sure: take this guitar.
It was what I wrote
'Corydon On Fire For Lovely Alexis' on.
and also
'Meliboeus Maybe (Whose Flock Do You Think This Is?)'

Mopsus said: Wow, thanks. Thanks!
You can have my crook, which Antigenes really wants,
but can't have: a long-tail question mark
in bronze and wood. It's yours.

Eclogue 6

Though *Eclogue 4* is more famous, *Eclogue* 6 has always struck me as the most extraordinary of the whole series—nothing less than an attempt to fuse the pastoral ideas of the mode with a genuinely epic sensibility. Vergil compresses an Ovidful of epic allusions into a few lines, and in doing so creates a high-tension masterpiece, stressed and instressed in almost every line with genesis, etiology and meaning. The fact that it also reflects back upon the business of being a poet, in this context, becomes more than merely a rhetorical trope. My guess is that this eclogue is the heart of the whole sequence, the place where the rural setting and Theocritan repurposings circle around the largest questions of national and poetic origins, such that they become the urbs surrounded and therefore situated by the rolling hills, woods and fields of the genre of which they are the capital.

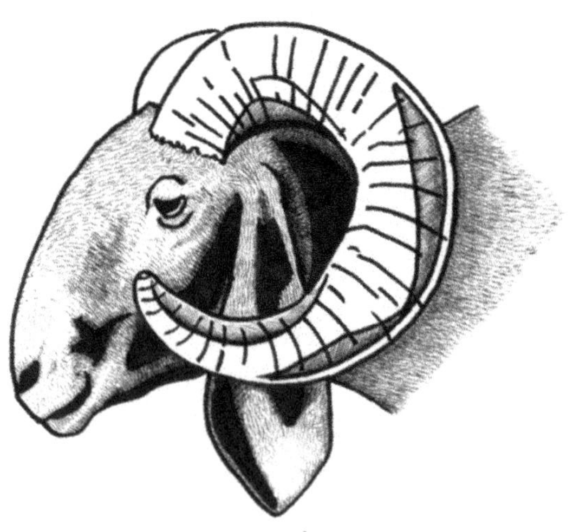

Eclogue 6

It began when I was in Sicily,
Mused-up to the gills
thinking of the old stories
and how the world was made.

Sicily maps a goat's head
straining its Italian leash to nibble Tunis:
it is chlorine-coloured woods,
a pallor of soil
the punishing sun
and there I was, staring at the perfect sea-blue
and thinking about writing my epic
when Apollo put his tongue in my ear
gave me the goddam common courtesy of a reach-around
and said: "keep your sheep plump, boyo
and your verse slender."

So I dropped a line to Varus:
he'd have to hire someone else to do the
praise-Varus-and-glorify-war thing.
Not that *I'll* be missed.
Put 'Varus' on the title page and we're in bestsellerland.
My name might as well be 'Remainder Stock'
for all the good it does sales.

Wait. Let me Irish-up this coffee,
which is to say, this poem,
with a slug of Pierian brand Muse.

Anyway, this happened: the boys
Chromis and Mnasyllos
broke into Silenus's house
found the old lecher asleep,
snoring like a waterfall,
veins thick as straining tendons,
brain still drenched in yesterday's wine,
out for the count;
a mug on its side next to him
screaming silently
and the whole of his room a mess of leaves
          and rotting petals.
So they BDSM'd him with ropes,
creepers, bindweed. Hog-tied.
It might've been sexy, I guess
but it wasn't. Real menace in their faces.
In swaggered Aegle,
white romper-suit, black boots and bowler,
cog-pattern mascara round one eye only,
and she landed a few blows,
smeared mush and paint on his face.
He was sobbing, begging, bruises
bursting with pain, his heart
kept banging on the door of cardiac arrest
desperate to be let inside.
"I'll do anything," he said, over and over,
like he was vomiting the words;
and "please", "I'm begging you, please"
and "please", as if that would sway them.
As if they weren't plenty pleased already.

We see animals running, grappling
other animals, teeth-to-nape,
and we think they're dancing.

We see the oaks in the wind
ponderously banging their heads
listening to a song only they can hear.

But not even Apollo can make Parnassus move.
Not even Orpheus can wipe the disdain
from the faces of Rhodope and Ismarus
filing their nails, tutting.

⁂

In the beginning
the huge world was disembarrassed of its void
by seeds flying
falling
inoculating earth and air and sea against nothingness;
and kindling, quick, into
hill-sized ocean swells of liquid fire
parabolas of elemental matter intersecting
spiralling and zoning-in
whirling into a solid globe
metal and stone baked together
and polished to cannonball smoothness
big enough to electroplate whole continents and seas
onto its surface.

Nereus, reeking of brine,
sopping seaweed dreadlocks
muscles like ribbed sand at low tide:
and he was locked away from the land.

The landscape rose like bread
under an oven sun

shunting clouds higher
they left their rain behind
and it fell down, or the land came up
hard to say which it was:
forests spread, and from up here
they looked like green-mould on the white fresh land.

Creatures twitched into frankenstein life
lurched over mountains
wholly uncomprehending of them.

Pyrhha threw stones
in the potter sense of the word,
wrung rock like a dishcloth
and the twisted braids became men and women.
Saturn in charge. Eagles from the Caucasus
with Nazi insignia on their wings
tuned friction's shriek into a slow crescendo
as they'd stuka down on Prometheus.

Sailors said: we lost touch with Hylas.
No idea where he is living now.
Doesn't seem to be even on social media.
I mean, we call out, and this new-solidified shoreline
bounces those soundwaves back, "Hylas! Hylas!
Where are you?" Zilch.

Pasiphaë's bestiality: never an easy sell.
On the other hand, this was no ordinary bull–white
as the virginity of Christ, powerfully built,
a good listener, placid eyed,
face white-lead-paint pale
ink-black ears two perfectly rounded parallelograms

haunches, thighs, cock, irresistible
Sure, it drove her mad. What lust doesn't?
Remember when Proteus's daughters
got punished for their pride?
made to believe they were all cows?
scrambling through the mud in all weathers
biting at grass, making moo.
Though they didn't go so far as
          actually fucking the bulls.
So, no luck for you girl.
You're on your own now, while he
lowers a vast expanse of white flank
onto an upholstery of purple hyacinths,
under that holly tree's crenulated shadow
chewing the colourless grass,
chatting-up some heifer from the populous herd.
And you're *shut it up, ladies,*
Dicte's ladies,
Lock down the whole forest,
Key-in the security code. Keep that bull in,
Maybe then I can track him down,
pick out line of coffee-bean patterns
where his hoofs have kicked divots from the lawn.
Maybe he's following the crowd. Or back at the stall. Girl, please.

Another woman, another obsession:
an apple, red-gold like a salmon's egg,
large and firm as a football,
from the Hesperides' sunset orchards.

Phaëthon's sisters' eczema
spread over their whole skin, and consolidated

into a crust of moss-coloured bark,
and when they next checked they were
birch trees, taller than ever before.

Gallus's cross-country run took him down by
the streams of Permessus, where
the officials, wearing luminous tabards,
redirected him by waving their IAAF rule books
sent him off up the Aonian hills,
and off he went,
panting in time to his heel-strikes on the dirt,
Phoebus's music in his ear-buds
though Linus was shouting after him,
really putting some welly into his voice,
face the colour of tizer, cords
of his neck tight as bass guitar strings,
yelling: "You forgot your Strat-o-caster, man!
The Muses's own Fender
the one the old Ascraean used to play,
those songs of his that made ash trees jig
and tumbledowned whole mountains.
Don't leave it behind, man!
Do the one about the birth of the Grynean wood,
rock and roll can never die, man.
Never die!"

We need to talk about sea-wolf Scylla.
Nisus was her father.
Her midriff belted around with
howling harrowing monsters
and she the Torpedo
the naval contact mine made flesh,
where the ships trail their wakes

from Ithaca to Sicily (my beloved Sicily)
until inadvertently easing their boats' chins
against the trigger
the tick-tick of contact
and a deep-bodied woof from
the dog throat of the whole sea
hurling up to spill back down
a shower of brine-rain, and turn
the waters a swirl of suck

a sailor's face swoops past you, and that's
terror you can see in his eyes.
But he's gone

down

to where it's always dark
and the water is dense with death
and the light never is.

Or Tereus, the glutton.
His abuse of young Philomela
stuck in his throat eventually.

Omnivorous Phoebus's Never Ending Tour
reworking his old songs
so that we barely recognise them
always on the road, always playing.
Eurotas in the mosh-pit, near the front
has all the lyrics by heart.
Silenus sings harmonies.
The stadium is so full it looks like
a curving valley forest
all these voices together flinging
songs at the stars,

till Vesper whispers the magic word
into the ears of every one of the sheep
and they all scuttle off, lock-hoof, clone herd,
and the day is folded away and stacked
in a storeroom whose walls and ceiling
are studded all over with twinkling stars.

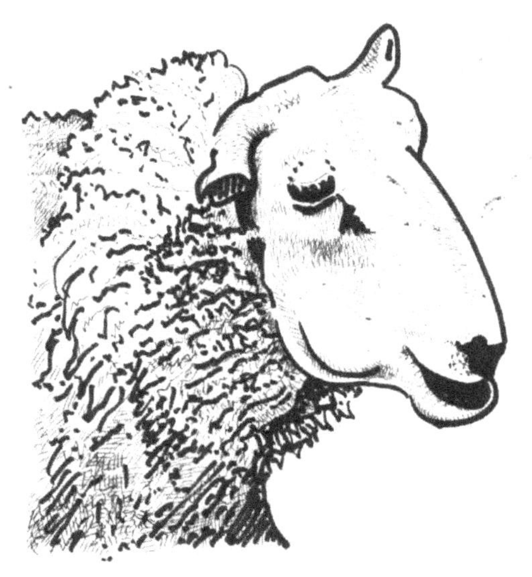

Eclogue 7

The third song-contest poem of the collection, this eclogue has puzzled many scholars, unsure whether we are actually supposed to take the to-and-fro as a serious competition. There seems little to choose between the two competitors, certainly, in terms of quality or approach, and the final judgment seems arbitrary. Critics try to find justification for it, but they fail to convince. The form is interesting too: 'because,' as Esmé E. Beyers notes, 'it is not really dramatic. All critics note that the singers do not themselves appear. Meliboeus introduces the words of the singers as he introduces Daphnis' words, and the text should dispense with the words Corydon Thyrsis alternately.' I have elected not to dispense with the names, though; although I have at least disposed the whole into a succession of more-or-less discrete pieces.

Eclogue 7

MELIBOEUS
A holm oak. Its throbbing leaves
a thousand vocal chords.
Foliage stacked as solidly
as the packed woolly humps of sheep
and the shaved white hides of goats
Thyrsis and Corydon's two flocks, driven together,
heads down, clustering around Daphnis,
as he sits under the whispering holm oak.

Thyrsis's sheep, Corydon's goats
udders rubber gloves milk-filled to
stretching point and tied off at the wrist.
The Arcadians are ready for the singing to start,
and I catch sight of Daphnis
and Daphnis sees me too, and he says:
come quick come here Meliboeus;
safe, at least. Safe inside.

Stow my flock in this shed through winter
straw dry as wood shavings
goats nibbling at the windows
fooled by the frost flowers on the glass
And Spring:
Cows come bumbling over the meadows
act like dipping-bird toys at the stream
The river is called Mincius and
his endless green shoulders
are epauletted with waving reeds.

Somebody told me that oak is sacred.
This very oak, hollow as an unworn coat.
Those crumbs flaking off it, and flying through the air?
Bees. And what could I do?
I had no Alcippe or Phyllis to look after the lambs,
milk still adhering around their mouths.

The match of Corydon against Thyrsis
was a mighty one. Annihilating.
It mattered more than work, than food, than sleep.

Hunting dogs in the heat, tongues out
like untucked shirt-tails.
Rose stems taloned with thorns.

The poem goes out as a single thing
Once lit, it makes a magnificent
firework flower of light;
in the sky. But of course it always falls back down
as fading neon crumbs and embers
that settle into hiding places in the grass
and are as invisible as the song that says

CORYDON
Libethra girls are lovely. But
Silence is a snooker-ball-sized shape
inside my mouth. Codrus rivals Apollo
I'll ornament the pine with my dangling lyre.

THYRSIS

It's raining in Arcady. The shepherds
look grim under the cowls of their raincoats.
Codrus's enSommed body looks trodden upon,
sides unstitched, greyblack offal spilling out.

CORYDON

A boar's severed head, skin like discarded carpet,
bristling, worn smooth in odd places by generations of feet
Young Micon heaves it to the Delian woman
together with the upended chandelier of a stag's antlers.
It's a gift offered in hope of good luck. He is shoeless.
Purple socks slipping on the polished marble.

THYRSIS

The milk in this bowl is as white as the morning star,
Dick Straightup, and these cakes are delicious.
The garden you surveil is a sanctuary for weeds.
You are a statue, and dark green landwrack
clutches your legs, all the mosses and lichens of Gothic,
but one day your statue will be untarnishable gold.

CORYDON

Honey brewed by bees from their thyme-fed spittle
is not so sweet on my tongue as is Galatea, child of Nereus
whiter than swans, smooth as the wax front of an ivy leaf.
Come to me. I am Corydon and I endorse this message.

Thyrsis
The taste of a herb so bitter it feels as if
your tongue has received an electric shock:
gorse-rough, vile-flavoured seaweed, year-long aftertaste.
Go home, grass-fed cows, for very shame, go home.

Corydon
Textured dark green towelling Is moss
on boulders by the springs, or meadow lawns
The wood of the strawberry trees is green
as the shadow it beams from the parching light.

Thyrsis
A stick dipped in pitch, the black glob
heartshaped and glistening, and set alight,
smoke-flame dusting the door's crime-scene with soot
The torrenting wind comes at us like a wolf after sheep.

Corydon
Junipers. Chestnut trees with hippy hairdos.
Fruit strewn over the ground, every one a locket
inside which is cached the song of songs.
And if Alexis goes, every river will dry.

Thyrsis
Grassblades stiff and dry as the reed of an unplayed clarinet.
Bacchus has a grudge against these hills. These dying vines.
Phyllis might sing the dead woodland green again.
Every rainstorm is the actual flesh and blood of God.

CORYDON
Poplars like pillars. They are dear to Alcides.
Bacchus loves the vines, grapes like clustered eyeballs
a teardrop of dew on each one. Phyllis loves the hazels.
And hazel out-trumps myrtle, even Apollo's laurel.

THYRSIS
The ash is the most beautiful tree in the woods.
The pine in the gardens, the poplar by rivers
The fir on mountaintops; but if you, lovely Lycidas,
Come often to me, ash and pine would yield to you.

MELIBOEUS
I remember everything.
I report everything.
Thyrsis struggled against his inevitable loss.
Corydon is the one. Our Corydon the winner.

Eclogue 8

Like the prophetic fourth eclogue, *Eclogue 8* is also addressed to Pollio, and is yet another song-contest between two shepherds. But this poem is unlike the other three that precede it as possible. My reading of it is that such notionally pastoral love poems, here, are the vehicle for two paired and dangerously complementary meditations on the way violence and power (the latter conceived in terms of magical capacity for domination, for compelling others) parse love as such. The way they do that, of course, is through sex, which can so easily become a violent and dominating matter. It is one of the most persistent and widely-believed errors of human life that violence simplifies situations. In fact, of course, the reverse is almost always the case: violence complexifies, sometimes monstrously. But we cling to the former belief, the lie of the Gordian knot, because we crave simplicity and we find the prospect of violence exciting and libidinous. It takes courage to see things truly.

Eclogue 8

For I will consider the pastoral Muse of Damon and
Alphesiboeus.
For the cows were so broadly amazed at their singing they
forgot even to graze.
For it hypnotised lynxes three two one and you're under.
For the rivers were rendered stony-astonished and they
stuttered like snakes and stopped flowing altogether.
For I will tell the story of the pastoral Muse of Damon and
Alphesiboeus.
though you are sailing dextrously past the hefty, sheared-off
coastal defensive blocks of Timavus.
though you are tacking laboriously through the Illyrian sea.
For you cannot be certain the day ever dawn when I will
tell your story.
For freedom to sing is not guaranteed in this world.
For who could ever be as good as Sophocles?
For you are where I begin.
For your reputation will end me.
For ivy twitches a nematode wriggle across your wide forehead.

For it was barely nightfall. Daylight's impetus had not
wholly drained from the sky.
For dew saturated the grass, like water in the lungs of
a drowned woman.
For the cutstring puppet of Damon was propped against
an olive trunk
and it sang, it sang:
"Wake up, morning star, sleepy head.
My love for promised Nysa is quite dead.
so I am dead.

Maenalan songs spurt from my pipe, if you know what I mean.

Maenalus made the woodland shudder.
Made Pan and shepherds clutch one another.
With a song of murder.
Maenalan songs spurt from my pipe, if you know what I mean.

Hard, Mopsus fucked Nysa then and there.
You think lovers won't stop and stare?
Griffins rape mares.

It's a new age. Here's an end to hope.
Wild dogs force deer's lips to the cup
Mospus! Light it up!

Here comes the bride! Here comes the bride!
Confetti sprays! Husband: she's yours to ride!
Jam your cock inside.
Maenalan songs spurt from my pipe, if you know what I mean.

Oeta startles the evening star into running off,
going into witness-protection.
Maenalan songs spurt from my pipe, if you know what I mean.

Married now, bitch? No escape.
Could've had me instead of that ape.
Cry me the river we're presently sitting beside.
You hated my face. You hated my beard.
You think any of your gods really cared?
Maenalan songs spurt from my pipe, if you know what I mean.

I've been stalking you. I lurked in the hedge.
Watched as you played with your little kid.

Stealing fruit from the orchard.
Man, I wanted you then and there
I was stiff as a rod. I stared, I stared
I hid.
Maenalan songs spurt from my pipe, if you know what I mean.

Love is psychosis. Tmarus's bare stones
Brain blanking heat. Distant Garamantes
No human infant.
Maenalan songs spurt from my pipe, if you know what I mean.

It was sociopathic Love taught a mother.
to drain her children's blood in murder.
That was hard core.
Maenalan songs spurt from my pipe, if you know what I mean.

But who was the guilty party here?
The mother, or the madness of desire?
I say the latter.
Maenalan songs spurt from my pipe, if you know what I mean.

Sheep hunt down wolves. Gold apples grow on oaks.
Alders bloom with daffodils. The rough barks
of tamarisks ooze honey-blood amber.
Oaks out-sing swans. Dumb loses to dumber.

Let Tityrus cosplay Orpheus in the woodland.
Or swim with dolphins dressed as Arion
Maenalan songs spurt from my pipe, if you know what I mean.

Let the fucking ocean swallow everything
Lowlands, forest, towns, everything.
Let it fucking all go down.

I'll stand on the summit of Everest and watch everything
swirl into the Apocalypse Sea, and when everything
has drowned I'll throw myself in.
My pipe is dry of Maenalan songs for now."

For this was Damon's song, unplugged, harsh.
For it made the river weep incoherently through its
        mouthful of mud.
For the Muses, being women, were not pleased.
For this reason, Alphesiboeus stood up, wearing his guitar
        like bodyarmour, and sang
and sang:

"Bring out water.
Wrap soft wool around this altar;
Burn fine-smelling herbs and pale frankincense,
Accompany my magic with this incense.
Set my lover's cold mind on fire.
Desire. Desire. Desire.
Come to me Daphnis, this magic spell will bring you home.

Dislodge the moon from its roulette-wheel spin.
Sing to draw it down.
Like Circe sang Ulysses' men into swine.
The cold snake in the meadows is torn outside-in,
the ripped string of its guts laid out clean
Come to me Daphnis, this magic spell will bring you home.

To tie you up I use three cords each a different colour.
To charm you I move your image three times around the altar.
Witch-magic works in threes.
The three knots Amaryllis weaves
iridesce as the colours change.

She is making magical lover's chains.
Come to me Daphnis, this magic spell will bring you home.

The clay hardens on my voodoo doll.
I hold this other one over flame as wax drops fall.
So may Daphnis melt with love for me!
Sprinkle some flour
on the fire.
Burn bay-leaves til they crackle
and blacken.
Daphnis burns; this burning leaf is Daphnis.
Come to me Daphnis, this magic spell will bring you home.

Daphnis will want me. He will yearn
On and on.
Like a long-horn heifer
who's been looking for a mate for, like, forever,
lost in the woods, collapsing by a stream
where the marsh sedges grow white and green
forlorn, forlorn, forlorn.
He will want me more and more.
Come to me Daphnis, this magic spell will bring you home.

He's a fucking traitor for leaving me, is the God's honest.
These mementos of the affair are all I have left.
I'll bury them in the soil to send the spell west.
Come to me Daphnis, this magic spell will bring you home.

These herbs are from Pontis.
I made these poisons myself. It was Moeris
who gave them me – they grow wild in Pontus.
By their aid I have with my own eyes seen Moeris
turn werewolf and lope into the wood.

And also call spirits from the dead.
And charm sown corn away from neighbouring farmstead.
Come to me Daphnis, this magic spell will bring you home.

Carry out the ashes, Amaryllis,
Throw them over your head into running water
And don't look back.
With their help I'll make Daphnis pay.
Come to me Daphnis, this magic spell will bring you home.

The ashes that were dead and desiccated and white
have of themselves rekindled and caught alight.
Now the flame shivers on the low altar
I could barely believe what my own eyes saw.
Hylax the dog is yapping at the door.
Is devours Seems.
Do lovers invent their own dreams?
Come to me Daphnis, this magic spell will bring you home."

Eclogue 9

This poem picks up the theme of the first eclogue: farmers and herdsmen displaced by the military, a reference either to the specific circumstances of Italy in the 40s and 30s BC, or else to a longer-term, perennial component of human life whereby the ones who do the work and grow the food are overpowered by those with the skill for neither but the wit to master techniques of overpowering.

As far as the translations go, two idioms are in play throughout: an unidiomatic, uncommon 'poetic' voice and something closer to, as Wordsworth put it, the language really used by men and women. The latter has its claim on pastoral because the mode is about the common people; but actually the former, particularly in its Hughesian granite mythology of the land version, is not so far as you might think either. In these last two translations the balance is deliberately tipped first the one way and then the other—or to be precise, first, here, the other way, and then, in '10,' the one.

Eclogue 9

LYCIDAS
Off, Moeris? Tramping to town?

MOERIS
It's a fucking welter, Lycidas.
We've lived long enough to see the unliving day.
        Clung to our little farm for a while, but now it's
        eviction.
A stranger says: "I own this, and you lot can fuck off."

Bashed. The cudgel on my naked back struck
        sparks from the cobbles of my spine
which is to sing the old song Chance The One True God.

We've sent the new master some kids as a gift;
        and each one is a matryoshka goat,
inside each curse a smaller curse, and inside that another.

LYCIDAS
Where the hills swell from the meadow's edge
rising to where the summit borders sky
        daytime moon like an owl's eye;
the ridge of the land dropping again
sloping down to the whorl of water;
the old beeches with their now shattered tops:
it was only the songs of your Menalcas that saved all that.

MOERIS
That's the story. An unmarked grave.
Songs are useless now,
        music tuneless and words are senseless.
Only the angled weapons of war makes sense, Lycidas.

We're silly doves, filling
Dodona's courtyard with coos
until the eagle comes:
swells, in the white sky,
from speck to
eye-filling blur
fluttery crescendo
fist-smash, on us,
hooks-for-hands
bundled onto the ends of two tight legs
grabbing, and his talon-beak
loosening our sinews and
the fibres of our muscles.
The beak fidgets, fidgets inside our breast,
and comes out red

Inside an wormeaten oak,
hollow as an unworn coat.
On the sinister side a raven
harshes its voice at me.

I took it as a warning, luckily.
It's why you're still alive, Moeris. Menalcas too.

LYCIDAS
Sad solace in poetry

Menalcas was almost torn from us. You too.

After the first prism levered the colours out of white
they never quite fitted back together again.
We call this "impurity". There will be
nobody left to sing about the women.

There will be red flower petals littering the ground
a bead-curtain of lineated green shade from the trees.

Slyly, I overheard you reciting the other day
plucking the ghost out of your darling Amaryllis:
"Tityrus, until I come back – the curt way – feed my goats,
Tityrus drive the herd to water,
watch for the he-goat
he butts with his horn."

MOERIS
Maybe you mean these fragmentary lines:

"Varus we know you want to flatten Mantua
Pound it with your ranked hefty smoothbores
Tenderise the ground to mud and craters:
We know it has strategic importance
as the key to unlucky Cremona.
Don't.
If you spare us, swans will applaud you,
clatter their tasselled elbows together
strike rainbows from their huge wings
and your name will float to the sun."

LYCIDAS
A swarm of bees puts all its voices
into one hairdryer cry of *refusal*
at the yews of Corsica.

Heifers process clover with mechanical mouths
inflate their udders like party balloons.

The Muses kitted me out in a poet's polyester uniform
paid me the poet's minimum wage.
I bussed songs to all the tables.

Customers were pleased to call me bard.
But I don't trust them.
I'm hardly sweet-swan-of-wherever
like Varius or Cinna.
I screech the black-wind frosty goose cackle.

MOERIS
That's exactly where I am, Lycidas,
silently turning it over in my mind, in case I can recall it.
A cool poem, too:

"Come with me Galatea.
Can pleasure live inside when all four walls are waves
        and roof a scruff of white foam?
The carpals and petals of roses are the emblem.

Spring scatters a chaff-cloud of flowers behind it,
a thousand colours in its trail, hoping to confuse
Winter's shrieking, ever-closer AIM-9 Sidewinder.
        as Autumn twists and hurtles.

White poplar bends over the cave.
The tangled fraying cables of vines.
Shadows recoil from the light.

Come with me Galatea,
A procession of newborn waves
wild as any baby,
bash their heads against the shore
desperate to suckle,
but doomed to break and die."

LYCIDAS
Not that one. The hypothermia one:

"Daphnis, staring yourself nightblind
at the tattered remnants of the old constellations rising.

Here, a luminous asterisk footnoting the whole black page
of the sky
That's Dionean Caesar's star.

Caesar smiling on the yellow bubble-wrap of cobbed corn
darkening the grape on the sunny hills.

Slit the veins of pears-twigs, Daphnis
and graft a cuckoo fruit onto the stem.
Your children's children's children will gather what you have
sown."

MOERIS
Time defrauds our bank accounts.
The Platonic form of identity theft is Time.

The angular rock of Memory
is pebbled by this stream, smooth as a tumour-stone.

When I was a boy I played that song on my bedside tape-
machine
through long summer evenings to send me to sleep.

Now my ears have forgotten all my songs.
My mouth has forgotten its own voice

The wolves see Moeris before he sees them,
They're a long way off, but their superpower
is annihilating distance, hurl distance behind them

all the time Moeris motionless
staring

Still, we can rely on Menalcas to remember your songs.
Often as you like.

LYCIDAS
The more you beg the more I want it.

The perfectly flat mesh of the ocean's surface.

The breeze that must move
to fulfil the bare definition of breeze:
it stops moving and becomes dead.

We're halfway to Bianor's remote tomb
you can see it in the distance,
coming into view.

Here, where farmers raise their shoehorn buzzsaws
and unleash their inner hauntings of wasps
to devour bough after bough:
here, Moeris, let us sing.

Here put down the kids.
We'll reach the town all the same.
Rain wrapped around a column of sleet
riddling such snow as remains.
Toads lurch across rain-drummed roads.
We can still sing, if we raise our voice.

I will relieve you of this burden.

Moeris
There is nothing more to say, lad.
There are jobs to do.
Our songs will sound better when the master himself has come.

Eclogue 10

Vergil's friend and old schoolfellow Cornelius Gallus (c. 70 - 26 BC) was himself also a poet, but more importantly for Vergil's connectivity to the corridors of power, important politician. The conceit of this poem is that Gallus has been deserted by his lover Lycoris and is dying, to the great sorrow of the natural world. Three gods come along to try to talk him out of his death, but to no avail. It's based, as several Vergilian Eclogues are, on Theocritus (in this case his first Idyll); but more to the point it paid itself forward, influence-wise, into many great poems, not least Shelley's mighty elegy 'Adonaïs' (1821). That latter poem seems to me the most impressive validation of Vergil's original that English poetry has produced. The Marie-Antoinette-dressed-as-a-shepherdess aspect of styling high-born Gallus as a humble shepherd invites us to take it seriously, I think. There are many working-class men who have spent some time in the army, and afterwards done one or other rural job, whose hearts have been broken by a woman, where our culture's imprisoning discourses of masculine toughness and taciturnity and so on push to breaking point.

Eclogue 10

This is the end.
Last task: frost dry as sandpaper
covering all external surfaces.
The wind biting at itself
        smouldering
Muse Arethusa's breath, passing into my lungs
fizzling out again over my tongue.

A shrunken poem.

Ghost grows solid for Gallus, humming its voltage
for Gallus:
impossible to refuse.

The river oms its trance
flows smokily down the trench of the world
to lose itself in the salt sea
        where Arethusa and Doris languidly copulate
in the drowned medium.

Gallus, the anxious lover.

Goats, snub-nosed, pistol-headed,
bury their faces in the hay
blow luminous tatters aside, chewing,
and all I do is sing
at the woodland's receptive curve,
one Jodrell Bank ear of green.

Where were you, all you single ladies
all you single ladies
when Gallus was was was *hysteric* with his unrequited love?
Put up your hands.
The scree-slopes of Parnassus;
Mount Pindus;
The waiting rooms of Aeonian Aganippe;
no excuses.

Laurel leaves squeezed teardrops
from their stomata,
meniscus
tight as drumskin.

Bruise-coloured tamarisk.

That huge hill called Maenalus with its
pelt of pines
became fragile as an eggshell with grief
for Gallus.
The sheep were shameless in sorrow,
their narrow skulls full of sap
curdcoloured fleeces heavy with rainwater
staring
an ice-age.
Handsome as Adonis was
he still fed his sheep beside the streams.

The shepherd came.
The swineherd came.
Menalcas came, sopping wet
        carrying cattle feed, a bucket of doused acorns.

Apollo came
dressed as a jazz trumpeter.
"Gallus," he wheezed, "you lost your fucking mind?
Your girl Lycoris, she gone, solid gone.
She gone over the range, man,
where the snow never melts, and the winds
are a vise crushing your head,
where your hands and feet get so cold
feel like Gestapo ripped out your fingernails and your toenails
forced you to wade boiling water.
She's a rather be there than here lady, my friend."

Silvanus came, leaves caught in his hair,
red and marmite-colour and whisky-yellow.

Pan came, Arcady's local god
his skin smeared with vermillion juice
crimson with squeezed elderberries
coloured like the devil from a mystery play,
and he said: "get over yourself, man.
Get the fuck over it."

Gallus sideeyed them all. "The fuck.
Tell it to the mountains.
Boo, and may I take this opportunity to add, hoo.
My bones would soften
        picked clean of flesh and soaked in vinegar nine weeks.
I could have shepherded *your* flocks,
I could have crushed the purple from the
        soggy baubles of *your* grapes
Phyllis; or Amyntas, with her skin

the colour of violets, cyan-black,
hyacinths,
my darling would be stretched alongside me;
vines would festoon our bedroom ceiling,
Phyllis yanking garlands from the tangle;
Amyntas singing.
But that wasn't to be.
You fall in love with who you fall in love with.

The trickling spring is cold
like void.
The meadows are soft as decay.
I would lie there with my lover until time
blissed me to dust.

But now to be a solider
comes on me like a persistent delusional psychosis:
in my body-armour
rifle lengthy as a spear
the god of war himself my recruiting sergeant:
flown overseas,
this shithole or that one, in the Middle-to-Far East,
where some bastard had left the furnace door open
and the furnace was the entire sky
and the least virile of breezes
stroked webs rolling down-dune
along the very toppermost surface of the sand.
And all this time she was in Germany,
fucking *Germany*,
Austria maybe,
Rhine water cold as the moon.

All that ice white ice-cream applied with a palette-knife
  to the tops of those Alps.
I could not fucking believe this.
Could not fucking even believe it.
I could have said, *darling don't let*
the frost nip your toes,
and I would almost not be being sarcastic.
Almost.

Going.
Going.

Go on. Let me have a tootle on that Sicilian flute
then
it's not as if I've never seen fucking woodland before
now
is it.
I've grafittized my name, tree-trunks for concrete walls;
  growing, growing, gone.
I'll link arm in arm with the nymphs and
goat-trip down that yellow brick road together
to emerald Maenalus,
or I'll hunt wild pigs in the wilderness.
No amount of icecrust on the soil will stop me.
I'm there already.
In my imagination, I mean.
I'm there.

Like that could solve my mental health issues.
Like the gods give a flying fuck for humanity.
Hamadryads don't put lead in my pencil.

Goodbye; its goodbye from me, it's a long goodbye from him.

Drink as much Hebrus as you like. Stand there
in the drizzle
shoeless;
watch the dishclout-coloured snow
get progressively acned by the winter rain. Then
say yah, yah to your sheep, and thwack
        their woolly withers with a switch

under the stars
as the constellation of the Crab looks away
to a more interesting portion of the sky.

Dying bark shrinks, cracks
on elms as tall as a window-cleaner's ladder;
and we cede the whole of the territory
that comprises us and is us
to Love
the Conqueror."

That's what the poet said.
He sat there, right where you're standing now,
and all the time
he braided flexible stems of hibiscus into
baskets. He was poeticizing about Gallus,
Gallus,
the much-loved

green

alder shoots in the sharpness of spring.
Time to go. The shade is poisonous to poets,
allergic to shadow.
Dusk falls through itself,
and the goats
jiggle and scramble and bleat their kazoo bleats
going home.

Appendix 1
An essay on Pastoral

☙ 1 ❧

We put culture on one side, bracketing with it society, architecture, religion, art and so on; and we put nature *waaaay* over the other side, there. Nature doesn't make culture, or so we believe. We make culture. Of course, nature makes us first (inevitably we are, in one sense, a product of nature). But once nature has made us we *go on* to make another thing, which I'm here calling culture. That two-step is essential to the form of distinction being made; and its doubleness is the structure of pastoral. The 'doubling' is what William Empson identified long ago as central to the mode.

I'm sure that is over-stark, as assertions go. Put it this way: does nature have culture? Nature may manifest society, or something close to it: the pack of dogs, the beehive. But does the beehive have culture? When the bees do their little dance, is that art? We're tempted to say no because the dance of bees is functional, and because we assume bees don't reflect upon the dance *as dance*. Presumably we believe that such self-reflection is needful for a performance to *be* art. But, really, how can we possibly know? What the bee-dance says to me is that our grasp of the natural world is defined, indeed is constituted, by a kind of existential paucity. It is what we cannot apprehend as culture that is the core of nature. In *The Beast in the Nursery* Adam Phillips says: 'we prefer the barbarity of culture to the barbarity of nature even though we usually can't tell them apart.' He adds a rather neat *after-all*: 'there is nothing more cultured than our fantasies about nature'. True, that.

Nature is always the resource that has always already been worked. The landscape is not 'nature'; it is what cultivation has made of the natural resource. Nature is worked, and therefore Pastoral is always reworked—practically speaking, an eclogue is always a reworking of Hughes as a reworking of Wordsworth as a reworking of Vergil as a reworking of Theocritus (for example). Pastoral is a kind of blockchain, and in a more acute and formally self-reflexive sense than the standard 'intertextuality' argument might suggest, the generalist insistence that all literature is a kind of blockchain. Pastoral is much more specifically so.

Pastoral as escape means that there is a benchmark existence from which escape looks both desirable and possible. This rather banal explanation, though, leads us into to some surprisingly complex and relevant places. At the risk of over-simplification, we might say: start from a position when life is hard, relentless—when life is work, and life is urban, and life is scarcity and frustration and ugliness—then fantasy becomes: ease, unobstruction, leisure, rural, abundant and satisfaction. This is the pastoral of Theocritus and Vergil and Spenser, the classic understanding of the *locus amoenus*. But something happens to pastoral in the 18th and early 19th centuries that rewires this, we can be honest, rather simplistic understanding. What's facile about it is the way it contains its own contradiction: a life that is all holiday is no holiday at all, since there's no benchmark of tedium and stress from which *to* escape, and it is the release, not the merely sensual pleasure, that is the key thing). The modification of pastoral entailed a two-step: first Goldsmith's *Deserted Village* (1770) and then Crabbe's *The Village* (1783) described rural life as hard, draining, frustrating and poor (as indeed it largely is) whilst insisting that *once upon a time* it had been golden, Arcadian. That is to say, they, and other poets from around this time doing similar things with the pastoral mode such as John Struthers, Clare and Balfour, were engaged in relocating the nature of Arcadia from being a different *place* to being a different (past) *time*. Instead of being defined as a (good) place distinct from the (bad) city or court, it becomes a good (past) *time* distinct from the bad present. That in turn connects with a longer tradition of 'past Golden Age' mythology. The fit, there, is so precise that pastoral itself can become seen as a mode of nostalgia, or more precisely as the faux-nostalgia of yearning for a time you never yourself actually experienced.

That's not right, though; because, after Vergil, the most important intervention into the pastoral tradition is Wordsworth's poetic creation of 'Nature' as a ground of transcendental aesthetic and ontological value—and Wordsworth's concept here flows directly from the 18th-century traditions of Goldsmithian or Crabbean 'anti-pastoral.' There could be plenty to say, as well, about how the erotics of pastoral blur into a masculinist desire to possess and control the Nature of both land and of women, which elides—particularly through the Victorian reception of Wordsworth—with a weirdly de-eroticised construction of 'purity' in Nature. This essay is long enough already, so I'm going to ask you to take it all on trust. You might trust less my insistence that it is from this new thing—I mean, from Wordsworth's new version of 'Nature'—that much of the force and a surprising number of the ethical and aesthetic specifics of modern-day environmentalism derive. It's true, though. I mean, I don't want to *over*state the influence; although, actually, it's hard to overstate the way the 19th century's most influential English-language poet shaped a whole culture, and the ways in which the later 20th-century

Green movements, in reacting against the machinism of early 20th-century Modernist and Popular cultures, inevitably reached back to something always-already Wordsworthian in their revalorisation of natural spaces.

Wordsworth is the second footprint in the 'two-step' I mentioned above. From pastoral as a pleasant Arcadian other-place we stride, first, to pastoral as a pleasant Arcadian vanished-time, to which the anti-pastoral of present-day rural suffering is contrasted; and second, we move to pastoral as a mode of transcendence *grounded in* contemporary rural suffering. Wordsworth's Michael (the hero of 'Michael: A Pastoral Poem') has grown very old in a life of ceaseless labour, physical restriction and hardship. But because it has always been a life in Nature, it has been an authentic existential experience of the kind unavailable equally to those to live in the town or the past:

> So lived he till his eightieth year was past.
> And grossly that man errs, who should suppose
> That the green Valleys, and the Streams and Rocks
> Were things indifferent to the Shepherd's thoughts.
> Fields, where with cheerful spirits he had breathed
> The common air; the hills, which he so oft
> Had climbed with vigorous steps; which had impressed
> So many incidents upon his mind
> Of hardship, skill or courage, joy or fear;
> Which like a book preserved the memory
> Of the dumb animals, whom he had saved,
> Had fed or sheltered, linking to such acts,
> So grateful in themselves, the certainty
> Of honorable gains; these fields, these hills,
> Which were his living Being, even more
> Than his own blood—what could they less? had laid
> Strong hold on his affections, were to him

A pleasurable feeling of blind love,
The pleasure which there is in life itself.

[Wordsworth, 'Michael', 61-77]

His son Luke goes into the town, and is instantly lost. Only by staying in the country can Michael stay strong, even to his death in his late 80s. Something similar is true of all of Wordsworth's rural poor: the Leech Gatherer, Cumberland beggar, even the mad woman in 'The Thorn'. Nature homes them, in a profound ur-Heideggerian sense, and that fact reconfigures the force of pastoral itself. To cut what is becoming an over-lengthy excursion short, I'll sketch a line straight from Wordsworth's natural world to the late-20th-century pastoral of Hughes's superb *Moortown* poems (1979): the jumping-off-point for the present volume.

I don't want, as I say, to labour the point. We need only touch on, say, *Moortown*'s 'Tractor' as one place where the pleasant sunny Arcadian wish-fulfilment of pastoral has come all the cold, hard way around to bite its own tail: not for transcendence, or even authenticity, but instead for a kind of valorisation of sheer endurance. It's the version of pastoral 'celebrated' (if that's the word) in Alejandro G. Iñárritu's 2015 movie *The Revenant*.

The tractor stands frozen—an agony
To think of. All night
Snow packed its open entrails. Now a head-pincering
    gale,
A spill of molten ice, smoking snow,
Pours into its steel.
At white heat of numbness it stands
In the aimed hosing of ground-level fieriness.

It defied flesh and won't start.
Hands are like wounds already
Inside armour gloves, and feet are unbelievable
As if the toe-nails were all just torn off.
I stare at it in hatred. Beyond it
The copse hisses—capitulates miserably
In the fleeing, failing light. Starlings,
A dirtier sleetier snow, blow smokily, unendingly, over
Towards plantations Eastward.
All the time the tractor is sinking
Through the degrees, deepening
Into its hell of ice.

What's particularly nice about this is the way Hughes uses a machine as a means of focusing the existential authenticity of post-Wordwsorthian pastoral. It's the right machine, of course, since modern farming could hardly happen without tractors. But still, there's a near-miraculous metamorphosis in the poem, in which an artefact of culture becomes, without slipping into any foolish pathetic fallacy, *nature itself*. Becomes, we might say, the objective correlative of Wordsworth's Michael's persistence, strength and labour. Out of hardship is generated beauty (for surely we can agree this is a very beautiful poem).

I don't know if there's a larger context here, which tracks the increasing pleasantness of general human existence against an increasing valorisation of hardship as such. If one's life is actually hard, one is less likely to enjoy the artistic representation of that hardship back upon yourself. The starving human finds no pleasure in contemplating going on a diet. If your life is basically comfortable, and your sufferings inward rather than outward, then hardship acquires greater appeal. I don't know: there may be a parallel with politics. When real life is living with an empty belly four days out of every seven, is being cold day after day and dying in your thirties, you'll follow the leader who promises to make your life easy. When seven days are defined by twenty-one square meals, and your home is heated and your death decades deferred, there is much more space, I suppose, for something like Weber's Protestant work ethic to take shape: for hardship to become romanticised as vocation, or as self-discovery, or as a badge of human belonging.

2

This leads me to think again about Empson, the critic who has probably done more to shape my attitudes towards pastoral than any other. I'm not only talking about *Some Versions of Pastoral* (1935), although I do think that study retains its relevance as well as its power. But many of its key ideas, such as the notion that the mere representation of rural pleasure is boring, are actually already present in his first book, *Seven Types of Ambiguity* (1930):

> It is this (in some sense conscious) clash between different modes of feeling which is the normal source of pleasure in pastoral; or, at any rate, in so far as pastorals fail to produce it, one may agree with Johnson and call them a bore.
>
> Thou shalt eat crudded cream
> All the year lasting,
> And drink the crystal stream
> Pleasant in tasting;

Whig and whey whilst thou lust
And brambleberries,
Pie-lids and pastry-crust,
Pears, plums, and cherries.
(ANON., *Oxford Book.*)

The delicacy of versification here (alliteration, balance of rhythm, and so forth) suggests both the scholar's trained apprehension and the courtier's experience of luxury; but it is of the brambleberry that he is an epicure; the subject forces into contact with these the direct gusto of a "swain." That all these good qualities should be brought together is a normal part of a good poem; indeed, it is a main part of the value of a poem, because they are so hard to bring together in life. But such a case as this is peculiar, because one is made to think of the different people separately; one cannot pretend to oneself that the author is the rustic he is impersonating; there is an element of wit in the first conception of the style.

(*Seven Types*, 114-15)

This formal relation between 'simple' and 'complex' ('putting the complex in the simple'—the closest thing *Some Types of Pastoral* offers as a nutshell-definition of pastoral itself—is in fact that action of *all* art, as Empson himself knows) stitches form to social relations. Pastoral not only represents but also embodies, and therefore enables, a coming-together of poor-simples and rich-sophisticates.

> The essential trick of the old pastoral, which was felt to imply a beautiful relation between rich and poor, was to make simple people express strong feelings (felt as the most universal subject, something fundamentally true about everybody) in learned and fashionable language .... The effect was in some degree to combine in the reader or author the merits of the two sorts; he was made to mirror in himself more completely the effective elements of the society he lived in. This was not a process that you could explain in the course of writing pastoral; it was already shown by the clash between style and theme, and to make the clash work in the right way (not become funny) the writer must keep up a firm pretence that he was unconscious of it.
> [*Some Versions*, 11-12]

According to George Watson 'Empson later insisted that his Marxism in the thirties and after–at least until the Communist revolution in China in 1949, which he witnessed–was more serious than his writings reveal, and *Some Versions* assumed the class analysis of society and the ideal status of the "proletariat".'[1] This is not untrue, although the point for Empson, at least in the *Some Versions of Pastoral* book, is always to bring the potential for social harmony back into the orientations of individual subjectivity. René Wellek puts forward a slightly more reductive reading.

> [The book's] subject is the collapse of the pastoral relation between the swain-hero and the sheep people. It is again the theme of the loss of community, of the presumed original unity which

[1] Watson, *The Literary Critics* (Hogarth 1986), 184.

> underlies Eliot's concept of history. Pastoral is used in a very wide sense: thus the first chapter discusses proletarian literature which Empson considers a covert pastoral. But even proletarian literature is used in a much wider sense than the usual one ... Proletarian art is pastoral. The old pastoral implied "a beautiful relation between rich and poor" [11] but this relation has broken down, and the old pastoral had been replaced by the mock pastoral, the comic variety at first. Both versions, straight and comic, are based on a double attitude of the artist to the worker ("I am in one way better, in another not so good"), and this may well recognize a permanent truth about the aesthetic situation. "To produce pure proletarian art the artist must be one with the worker; this is impossible, not for political reasons, but because the artist never is at one with any public." [15][2]

Wellek might have added, though he doesn't, that this is a peculiarly Romantic version of 'the artist,' which itself problematises the case being made (something of which Empson himself was aware: 'Mob thought may kill us all before our time, but the scientist's view of it should not be warped by horror, and the writer who isolates himself from all feeling for his audience acquires the faults of romanticism without its virtues'). Actually, the implied individualism of all this is central to what Empson is arguing: not that the poet is alienated from society, but precisely that the (simple) poet holds within him/herself the (complex) of society. Here's Paul Alpers:

---

[2] Wellek, *A History of Modern Criticism 1750-1950: V English Criticism 1900-1950* (Yale 1986), 280.

> Marvell and Milton represent for Empson a withdrawal—to quote the verses that prompt the essay on 'The Garden'—of the mind into its own happiness. The strengths of the "old pastoral" are most fully manifest in Elizabethan works, particularly the dramas, which are discussed in the chapter on "Double Plots." The Elizabethan double plot is a version of pastoral, because it is a convention—the strongest and most capacious, it would seem, in all our literature—for the stable presentation of conflicts and contradictions and for putting the complexities of life into the "simple" effects of art.[3]

To quote the man himself: 'in pastoral you take a limited life and pretend it is the full and normal one, and a suggestion that one must do this with all life, because the normal is itself limited, is easily put into the trick though not necessary to its power' [*Some Versions of Pastoral*, 114]. The element that's missing here is the way paucity, and poverty, can become precisely the focus for *strength* in this reading of Nature.

Nature is, after all, so much bigger than we are. To switch back to Hughes, at the close of 'Examination at the Womb-Door', it is the potency of finitude, and not the pretense of fullness, that sounds in Crow's superbly insouciant 'Me, evidently'. It's a brutal and complex poem, and another key late 20th-century pastoral. It stages a process of control—the inspection, evaluation, and limitation of life—within female reproductive anatomy in a way which spills far beyond its control. What is really Arcadian is always *that we have survived this far at all.*

---

[3] Alpers, 'Empson on Pastoral', *New Literary History* 10:1 (1978) 112.

Who owns those scrawny little feet?   *Death.*
Who owns this bristly scorched-looking face?   *Death.*
Who owns these still-working lungs?   *Death.*
Who owns this utility coat of muscles?   *Death.*
Who owns these unspeakable guts?   *Death.*
Who owns these questionable brains?   *Death.*
All this messy blood?   *Death.*
These minimum-efficiency eyes?   *Death.*
This wicked little tongue?   *Death.*
This occasional wakefulness?   *Death.*

Given, stolen, or held pending trial?
Held.

Who owns the whole rainy, stony earth?   *Death.*
Who owns all of space?   *Death.*

Who is stronger than hope?   *Death.*
Who is stronger than the will?   *Death.*
Stronger than love?   *Death.*
Stronger than life?   *Death.*

But who is stronger than Death?

Me, evidently.

Pass, Crow.

It probably speaks to a continuing adolescence in my aesthetic sense, but by thunder I *love* that poem.

Appendix 2

Latin

I. MELIBOEUS, TITYRUS.

M. TITYRE, tu patulae recubans sub tegmine fagi / silvestrem tenui Musam meditaris avena; / nos patriae fines et dulcia linquimus arva: / nos patriam fugimus; tu, Tityre, lentus in umbra / formosam resonare doces Amaryllida silvas. / *T.* O Meliboee, deus nobis haec otia fecit: / namque erit ille mihi semper deus; illius aram / saepe tener nostris ab ovilibus imbuet agnus. / Ille meas errare boves, ut cernis, et ipsum / ludere, quae vellem, calamo permisit agresti / M. Non equidem invideo; miror magis: undique totis / usque adeo turbatur agris. En, ipse capellas / protinus aeger ago; hanc etiam vix, Tityre, duco: / hic inter densas corylos modo namque gemellos, / spem gregis, ah, silice in nuda conixa reliquit. / Saepe malum hoc nobis, si mens non laeva fuisset, / de caelo tactas memini praedicere quercus:— / [saepe sinistra cava praedixit ab ilice cornix.] / Sed tamen, iste deus qui sit, da, Tityre, nobis. / *T.* Urbem, quam dicunt Romam, Meliboee, putavi / stultus ego huic nostrae similem, quo saepe solemus / pastores ovium teneros depellere fetus: / sic canibus catulos similis, sic matribus haedos / noram, sic parvis componere magna solebam: / verum haec tantum alias inter caput extulit urbes, / quantum lenta solent inter viburna cupressi. / M. Et quae tanta fuit Romam tibi causa videndi? / *T.* Libertas; quae sera, tamen respexit inertem, / candidior postquam tondenti barba cadebat; / respexit tamen, et longo post tempore venit, / postquam nos Amaryllis habet, Galatea reliquit: / namque, fatebor enim, dum me Galatea tenebat, / nec spes libertatis erat, nec cura peculi: / quamvis multa meis exiret victima saeptis, / pinguis et ingratae premeretur caseus urbi, / non umquam gravis aere domum mihi dextra redibat. / M. Mirabar, quid maesta deos, Amarylli, vocares, / cui pendere sua patereris in arbore poma: / Tityrus hinc aberat. Ipsae te, Tityre, pinus, / ipsi te fontes, ipsa haec arbusta vocabant. / *T.* Quid facerem? Neque servitio me exire licebat, / nec tam praesentis alibi cognoscere divos. / hic illum vidi iuvenem, Meliboee, quot annis / bis senos cui nostra dies altaria fumant; / hic mihi responsum primus dedit ille petenti: / 'pascite, ut ante, boves, pueri, submittite tauros.' / M. Fortunate senex, ergo tua rura manebunt, / et tibi magna satis, quamvis lapis omnia nudus / limosoque palus obducat pascua iunco! / Non insueta gravis temptabunt pabula fetas, / nec mala vicini pecoris contagia laedent. / Fortunate senex, hic, inter flumina nota / et fontis sacros, frigus captabis opacum! / hinc tibi, quae semper, vicino ab limite, saepes / Hyblaeis apibus florem depasta salicti / saepe levi somnum suadebit inire susurro; / hinc alta sub rupe canet frondator ad auras; / nec tamen interea raucae, tua cura, palumbes, / nec gemere aeria cessabit turtur ab ulmo. / T. Ante leves ergo pascentur in aequore cervi, / et freta destituent nudos in litore pisces, / ante pererratis amborum finibus exsul / aut Ararim Parthus bibet, aut Germania Tigrim, / quam nostro illius labatur pectore voltus. / M. At nos hinc alii sitientis ibimus Afros, / pars Scythiam et rapidum Cretae veniemus Oaxen, / pauperis toto divisos orbe Britannos. / En umquam patrios longo post tempore finis, / pauperis et tuguri congestum caespite culmen, / post aliquot mea regna videns mirabor aristas? / Impius haec tam culta novalia miles habebit, / barbarus has segetes? En, quo discordia civis / produxit miseros! His nos consevimus agros! / Insere nunc, Meliboee, piros, pone ordine vitis. / Ite meae, felix quondam pecus, ite capellae. / Non ego vos posthac, viridi proiectus in antro, / dumosa pendere procul de rupe videbo; / carmina nulla canam; non, me pascente, capellae, / florentem cytisum et salices carpetis amaras. / T. Hic tamen hanc mecum poteras requiescere noctem / fronde super viridi: sunt nobis mitia poma, / castaneae molles, et pressi copia lactis; / et iam summa procul villarum culmina fumant, / maioresque cadunt altis de montibus umbrae.

II.

FORMOSUM pastor Corydon ardebat Alexim, / delicias domini, nec quid speraret habebat; / tantum inter densas, umbrosa cacumina, fagos / adsidue veniebat. Ibi haec incondita solus / montibus et silvis studio iactabat inani: / O crudelis Alexi, nihil mea carmina curas? / Nil nostri miserere? Mori me denique coges. / nunc etiam pecudes umbras et frigora captant; / nunc viridis etiam occultant spineta lacertos, / Thestylis et rapido fessis messoribus aestu / alia serpyllumque herbas contundit olentis. / at mecum raucis, tua dum vestigia lustro, / sole sub ardenti resonant arbusta cicadis. / Nonne fuit satius tristis Amaryllidis iras / atque superba pati fastidia, nonne Menalcan, / quam vis ille niger, quamvis tu candidus esses? / o formose puer, nimium ne crede colori! / alba ligustra cadunt, vaccinia nigra leguntur. / Despectus tibi sum, nec qui sim quaeris, Alexi, / quam dives pecoris, nivei quam lactis abundans. / mille meae Siculis errant in montibus agnae; / lac mihi non aestate novum, non frigore defit; / canto quae solitus, si quando armenta vocabat, / Amphion Dircaeus in Actaeo Aracimtho. / Nec sum adeo informis: nuper me in litore vidi, / cum placidum ventis staret mare; non ego Daphnim / iudice te metuam, si numquam fallit imago. / O tantum libeat mecum tibi sordida rura / atque humilis habitare casas, et figere cervos, / haedorumque gregem viridi compellere hibisco! / Mecum una in silvis imitabere Pana canendo.

/ Pan primus calamos cera coniungere pluris / instituit; Pan curat ovis oviumque magistros. / Nec te paeniteat calamo trivisse labellum: / haec eadem ut sciret, quid non faciebat Amyntas? / est mihi disparibus septem compacta cicutis / fistula, Damoetas dono mihi quam dedit olim, / et dixit moriens: 'Te nunc habet ista secundum.' / dixit Damoetas, invidit stultus Amyntas. / Praeterea duo, nec tuta mihi valle reperti, / capreoli, sparsis etiam nunc pellibus albo, / bina die siccant ovis ubera; quos tibi servo: / iam pridem a me illos abducere Thestylis orat; / et faciet, quoniam sordent tibi munera nostra. / Huc ades, O formose puer: tibi lilia plenis / ecce ferunt Nymphae calathis; tibi candida Nais, / pallelltis violas et summa papavera carpens, / narcissum et florem iungit bene olentis anethi; / tum casia atque aliis intexens suavibus herbis, / mollia luteola pingit vaccinia calta. / Ipse ego cana legam tenera lanugine mala, / castaneasque nuces, mea quas Amaryllis amabat; / addam cerea pruna: honos erit huic quoque pomo; / et vos, O lauri, carpam, et te, proxima myrte, / sic positae quoniam suavis miscetis odores. / Rusticus es, Corydon: nec munera curat Alexis, / nec, si muneribus certes, concedat Iollas. / Heu, heu, quid volui misero mihi! Floribus austrum / perditus et liquidis inmisi fontibus apros. / Quem fugis, ah, demens? Habitarunt di quoque silvas, / Dardaniusque Paris. Pallas, quas condidit arces, / ipsa colat; nobis placeant ante omnia silvae. / Torva leaena lupum sequitur; lupus ipse capellam; / florentem cytisum sequitur lasciva capella; / te Corydon, o Alexi: trahit sua quemque voluptas. / Aspice, aratra iugo referunt suspensa iuvenci, / et sol crescentis decedens duplicat umbras: / me tamen urit amor; quis enim modus adsit amori? / Ah, Corydon, Corydon, quae te dementia cepit! / Semiputata tibi frondosa vitis in ulmo est; / quin tu aliquid saltem potius, quorum indiget usus, / viminibus mollique paras detexere iunco? / Invenies alium, si te hic fastidit, Alexim.

III. MENALCAS, DAMOETAS, PALAEMON

M. DIC mihi, Damoeta, cuium pecus, an Meliboei? / *D.* Non, verum Aegonis; nuper mihi tradidit Aegon. / M. Infelix o semper, ovis, pecus, ipse Neaeram / dum fovet, ac ne me sibi praeferat illa veretur, / hic alienus ovis custos bis mulget in hora, / et sucus pecori et lac subducitur agnis. / *D.* Parcius ista viris tamen obicienda memento: / novimus et qui te, transversa tuentibus hircis, / et quo— sed faciles Nymphae risere—sacello. / M. Tum, credo, cum me arbustum videre Miconis / atque mala vitis incidere falce novellas. / *D.* Aut hic ad veteres fagos cum Daphnidis arcum / fregisti et calamos quae tu, perverse Menalca, / et cum vidisti puero donata, dolebas, / et si non aliqua nocuisses, mortuus esses. / M. Quid domini faciant, audent cum talia fures! / non ego te vidi Damonis, pessime, caprum / excipere insidiis, multum latrante Lycisca? / et cum clamarem: 'Quo nunc se proripit ille? / Tityre, coge pecus,' tu post carecta latebas. / *D.* An mihi cantando victus non redderet ille / quem mea carminibus meruisset fistula caprum? / Si nescis, meus ille caper fuit; et mihi Damon / ipse fatebatur, sed reddere posse negabat. / M. Cantando tu illum, aut umquam tibi fistula cera / iuncta fuit? Non tu in triviis, indocte, solebas / stridenti miserum stipula disperdere carmen? / *D.* Vis ergo inter nos quid possit uterque vicissim / experiamur? Ego hanc vitulam—ne forte recuses, / bis venit ad mulctram, binos alit ubere fetus— / depono: tu dic, mecum quo pignore certes. / M. De grege non ausim quicquam deponere tecum. / Est mihi namque domi pater, est iniusta noverca; / bisque die numerant ambo pecus, alter et haedos. / Verum, id quod multo tute ipse fatebere maius, / insanire libet quoniam tibi, pocula ponam / fagina, caelatum divini opus Alcimedontis; / lenta quibus torno facili superaddita vitis / diffusos hedera vestit pallente corymbos: / in medio duo signa, Conon, et—quis fuit alter, / descripsit radio totum qui gentibus orbem, / tempora quae messor, quae curvus arator haberet? / Necdum illis labra admovi, sed condita servo. / *D.* Et nobis idem Alcimedon duo pocula fecit, / et molli circum est ansas amplexus acantho, / Orpheaque in medio posuit silvasque sequentis. / Necdum illis labra admovi, sed condita servo: / si ad vitulam spectas, nihil est quod pocula laudes. / M. Nunquam hodie effugies; veniam, quocumque vocari / audiat haec tantum—vel qui venit ecce Palaemon / efficiam posthac ne quemquam voce lacessas. / *D.* Quin age, si quid habes, in me mora non erit ulla, / nec quemquam fugio: tantum, vicine Palaemon, / sensibus haec imis, res est non parva, reponas. / P. Dicite, quandoquidem in molli consedimus herba: / et nunc omnis ager, nunc omnis parturit arbos, / nunc frondent silvae, nunc formosissimus annus. / Incipe, Darmoeta; tu deinde sequere Menalca: / alternis dicetis; amant alterna Camenae. / *D.* Ab Iove principium, Musae; Iovis omnia plena: / ille colit terras, illi mea carmina curae. / M. Et me Phoebus amat; Phoebo sua semper apud me / munera sunt, lauri et suave rubens hyacinthus. / *D.* Malo me Galatea petit, lasciva puella, / et fugit ad salices, et se cupit ante videri. / M. At mihi sese offert ultro, meus ignis, Amyntas, / notior ut iam sit canibus non Delia nostris. / *D.* Parta meae Veneri sunt munera: namque notavi / ipse locum, aeriae quo congessere palumbes. / M. Quod potui, puero silvestri ex arbore lecta / aurea mala decem misi; cras altera mittam. / *D.* O quotiens et quae nobis Galatea locuta est! / partem aliquam, venti, divom referatis ad auris! / M. Quid prodest, quod me ipse animo non spernis, Amynta. / si, dum tu sectaris apros, ego retia servo? / *D.* Phyllida mitte mihi: meus est natalis, Iolla; / cum faciam vitula pro frugibus, ipse venito. / M. Phyllida amo ante alias; nam me discedere flevit, / et longum 'formose, vale, vale,' inquit, 'Iolla.' / *D.* Triste lupus stabulis, maturis frugibus imbres. / arboribus venti, nobis Amaryllidis irae. / M. Dulce satis umor, depulsis arbutus haedis, / lenta salix feto pecori, mihi solus Amyntas. / *D.* Pollio amat nostram, quamvis est rustica, Musam: / Pierides vitulam lectori pascite vestro. / M. Pollio et ipse facit nova carmina: pascite taurum, / iam cornu petat et pedibus qui spargat arenam. / *D.* Qui te, Pollio, amat, veniat quo te quoque gaudet: / mella fluant illi, ferat et rubus asper amomum. / M. Qui Bavium non odit, amet tua carmina, Maevi, / atque idem iungat vulpes et mulgeat hircos. / *D.* Qui legitis flores et humi nascentia fraga, / frigidus, O pueri, fugite hinc, latet anguis in herba. / M. Parcite, oves, nimium procedere; non bene ripae / creditur; ipse aries etiam nunc vellera siccat. / *D.* Tityre, pascentes a flumine reice capellas: / ipse ubi tempus erit, omnis in fonte lavabo. / M. Cogite ovis, pueri; si lac praeceperit aestus, / ut nuper, frustra pressabimus ubera palmis. / *D.* Heu, heu, quam pingui macer est mihi taurus in ervo! / Idem amor exitium est pecori pecorisque magistro. / M. His certe neque amor causa est; vix ossibus haerent. / nescio quis teneros oculus mihi fascinat agnos. / *D.* Dic, quibus in terris—et eris mihi magnus Apollo— / tris pateat caeli spatium non amplius ulnas. / M. Dic, quibus in terris inscripti nomina regum / nascantur flores, et Phyllida solus habeto. / P. Non nostrum inter vos tantas componere lites. / Et vitula tu dignus, et hic, et quisquis amores / aut metuet dulces, aut experietur amaros. / Claudite iam rivos, pueri, sat prata biberunt.

IV.

SICELIDES Musae, paulo maiora canamus! / Non omnis arbusta iuvant humilesque myricae; / si canimus silvas, silvae sint consule dignae. / Ultima Cumaei venit iam carminis aetas; / magnus ab integro saeclorum nascitur ordo: / iam redit et Virgo, redeunt Saturnia regna; / iam nova progenies caelo demittitur alto. / Tu modo nascenti puero, quo ferrea primum / desinet ac toto surget gens aurea mundo, / casta fave Lucina: tuus iam regnat Apollo. / Teque adeo decus hoc aevi te consule inibit, / Pollio, et incipient magni procedere menses. / te duce, si qua manent sceleris vestigia nostri, / inrita perpetua solvent formidine terras. / ille deum vitam accipiet, divisque videbit / permixtos heroas, et ipse videbitur illis, / pacatumque reget patriis virtutibus orbem. / At tibi prima, puer, nullo munuscula cultu / errantis hederas passim cum baccare tellus / mixtaque ridenti colocasia fundet acantho. / Ipsae lacte domum referent distenta capellae / ubera, nec magnos metuent armenta leones; / ipsa tibi blandos fundent cunabula flores, / occidet et serpens, et fallax herba veneni / occidet, Assyrium volgo nascetur amomum. / at simul heroum laudes et facta parentis / iam legere et quae sit poteris cognoscere virtus, / molli paulatim flavescet campus arista, / incultisque rubens pendebit sentibus uva, / et durae quercus sudabunt roscida mella / Pauca tamen suberunt priscae vestigia fraudis, / quae temptare Thetim ratibus, quae cingere muris / oppida, quae iubeant telluri infindere sulcos: / alter erit tum Tiphys, et altera quae vehat Argo / delectos Heroas; erunt etiam altera bella, / atque iterum ad Troiam magnus mittetur Achilles. / Hinc, ubi iam firmata virum te fecerit aetas, / cedet et ipse mari vector, nec nautica pinus / mutabit merces: omnis feret omnia tellus: / non rastros patietur humus, non vinea falcem; / robustus quoque iam tauris iuga solvet arator; / nec varios discet mentiri lana colores: / ipse sed in pratis aries iam suave rubenti / murice, iam croceo mutabit vellera luto; / sponte sua sandyx pascentis vestiet agnos. / Talia saecla, suis dixerunt, currite, fusis / concordes stabili fatorum numine Parcae. / Adgredere o magnos—aderit iam tempus—honores, / cara deum suboles, magnum Iovis incrementum! / Aspice convexo nutantem pondere mundum, / terrasque tractusque maris caelumque profundum! / Aspice, venturo laetentur ut omnia saeclo! / O mihi tam longae maneat pars ultima vitae, / spiritus et quantum sat erit tua dicere facta! / Non me carminibus vincet nec Thracius Orpheus, / nec Linus, huic mater quamvis atque huic pater adsit, / Orphei Calliopea, Lino formosus Apollo, / Pan etiam, Arcadia mecum si iudice certet, / Pan etiam Arcadia dicat se iudice victum. / Incipe, parve puer, risu cognoscere matrem, / matri longa decem tulerunt fastidia menses. / Incipe, parve puer, cui non risere parentes, / nec deus hunc mensa, dea nec dignata cubili est.

V. MENALCAS, MOPSUS

Me. CUR non, Mopse, boni quoniam convenimus ambo, / tu calamos inflare levis, ego dicere versus, / hic corylis mixtas inter consedimus ulmos? / *Mo.* Tu maior; tibi me est aequum parere, Menalca, / sive sub incertas zephyris motantibus umbras, / sive antro potius succedimus: aspice, ut antrum / silvestris raris sparsit labrusca racemis. / *Me.* Montibus in nostris solus tibi certat Amyntas. / *Mo.* Quid, si idem certet Phoebum superare canendo? / *Me.* Incipe, Mopse, prior, si quos aut Phyllidis ignes, / aut Alconis habes laudes, aut iurgia Codri: / incipe, pascentis servabit Tityrus haedos. / *Mo.* Immo haec, in viridi nuper quae cortice fagi / carmina descripsi et modulans alterna notavi, / experiar, tu deinde iubeto ut certet Amyntas. / *Me.* Lenta salix quantum pallenti cedit olivae, / puniceis humilis quantum saliunca rosetis, / iudicio nostro tantum tibi cedit Amyntas. / sed tu desine plura, puer; successimus antro. /
Mo. Extinctum nymphae crudeli funere Daphnim / flebant; vos coryli testes et flumina nymphis; / cum

complexa sui corpus miserabile nati, / atque deos atque astra vocat crudelia mater. / Non ulli pastos illis egere diebus / frigida, Daphni, boves ad flumina; nulla neque amnem / libavit quadrupes, nec graminis attigit herbam. / Daphni, tuum Poenos etiam ingemuisse leones / interitum montesque feri silvaeque loquuntur. / Daphnis et Armenias curru subiungere tigres / instituit; Daphnis thiasos inducere Bacchi, / et foliis lentas intexere mollibus hastas. / Vitis ut arboribus decori est, ut vitibus uvae, / ut gregibus tauri, segetes ut pinguibus arvis, / tu decus omne tuis. Postquam te fata tulerunt, / ipsa Pales agros atque ipse reliquit Apollo. / Grandia saepe quibus mandavimus hordea sulcis, / infelix lolium et steriles nascuntur avenae; / pro molli viola, pro purpureo narcisso, / carduus et spinis surgit paliurus acutis. / Spargite humum foliis, inducite fontibus umbras, / pastores, mandat fieri sibi talia Daphnis; / et tumulum facite, et tumulo superaddite carmen: / DAPHNIS EGO IN SILVIS HINC VSQUE AD SIDERA NOTVS / FORMONSI PECORIS CVSTOS FORMONSIOR IPSE. / *Me.* Tale tuum carmen nobis, divine poeta, / quale sopor fessis in gramine, quale per aestum / dulcis aquae saliente sitim restinguere rivo: / nec calamis solum aequiparas, sed voce magistrum. / [Fortunate puer, tu nunc eris alter ab illo.] / Nos tamen haec quocumque modo tibi nostra vicissim / dicemus, Daphnimque tuum tollemus ad astra; / Daphnin ad astra feremus: amavit nos quoque Daphnis. / *Mo.* An quicquam nobis tali sit munere maius / Et puer ipse fuit cantari dignus, et ista / iam pridem Stimichon laudavit carmina nobis. / *Me.* Candidus insuetum miratur limen Olympi, / sub pedibusque videt nubes et sidera Daphnis. / ergo alacris silvas et cetera rura voluptas / Panaque pastoresque tenet, Dryadasque puellas; / nec lupus insidias pecori, nec retia cervis / ulla dolum meditantur: amat bonus otia Daphnis. / ipsi laetitia voces ad sidera iactant / intonsi montes; ipsae iam carmina rupes, / ipsa sonant arbusta: 'Deus, deus ille, Menalca.' / Sis bonus O felixque tuis! En quattuor aras: / ecce duas tibi, Daphni, duas altaria Phoebo. / pocula bina novo spumantia lacte quotannis, / craterasque duo statuam tibi pinguis olivi, / et multo in primis hilarans convivia Baccho,— / ante focum, si frigus erit, si messis, in umbra,— / vina novum fundam calathis Ariusia nectar. / cantabunt mihi Damoetas et Lyctius Aegon; / saltantis satyros imitabitur Alphesiboeus. / Haec tibi semper erunt, et cum solemnia vota / reddemus Nymphis, et cum lustrabimus agros. / Dum iuga montis aper, fluvios dum piscis amabit, / dumque thymo pascentur apes, dum rore cicadae, / semper honos nomenque tuum laudesque manebunt; / ut Baccho Cererique, tibi sic vota quotannis / agricolae facient: damnabis tu quoque votis. / *Mo.* Quae tibi, quae tali reddam pro carmine dona? / Nam neque me tantum venientis sibilus austri, / nec percussa iuvant fluctu tam litora, nec quae / saxosas inter decurrunt flumina valles. / *Me.* Hac te nos fragili donabimus ante cicuta: / haec nos, 'Formosum Corydon ardebat Alexim,' / haec eadem docuit, 'Cuium pecus, an Meliboei?' / *Mo.* At tu sume pedum, quod, me cum saepe rogaret, / non tulit Antigenes—et erat tum dignus amari— / formosum paribus nodis atque aere, Menalca.

VI.

PRIMA Syracosio dignata est ludere versu, / nostra nec erubuit silvas habitare Thalia. / Cum canerem reges et proelia, Cynthius aurem / vellit, et admonuit: 'Pastorem, Tityre, pinguis / pascere oportet ovis, deductum dicere carmen.' / Nunc ego—namque super tibi erunt, qui dicere laudes, / Vare, tuas cupiant, et tristia condere bella— / agrestem tenui meditabor arundine Musam. / Non iniussa cano: si quis tamen haec quoque, si quis / captus amore leget, te nostrae, Vare, myricae, / te nemus omne canet; nec Phoebo gratior ulla est, / quam sibi quae Vari praescripsit pagina nomen. / Pergite, Pierides! Chromis et Mnasyllos in antro / Silenum pueri somno videre iacentem, / inflatum hesterno venas, ut semper, Iaccho: / serta procul tantum capiti delapsa iacebant, / et gravis attrita pendebat cantharus ansa. / Adgressi—nam saepe senex spe carminis ambo / luserat—iniciunt ipsis ex vincula sertis: / addit se sociam, timidisque supervenit Aegle,— / Aegle, Naiadum pulcherrima,—iamque videnti / sanguineis frontem moris et tempora pingit. / Ille dolum ridens, 'Quo vincula nectitis?' inquit; / 'solvite me, pueri; satis est potuisse videri: / carmina, quae voltis, cognoscite; carmina vobis, / huic aliud mercedis erit.' Simul incipit ipse. / Tum vero in numerum Faunosque ferasque videres / ludere, tum rigidas motare cacumina quercus; / nec tantum Phoebo gaudet Parnasia rupes, / nec tantum Rhodope miratur et Ismarus Orphea. / Namque canebat, uti magnum per inane coacta / semina terrarumque animaeque marisque fuissent, / et liquidi simul ignis; ut his exordia primis / omnia et ipse tener mundi concreverit orbis; / tum durare solum et discludere Nerea ponto / coeperit, et rerum paulatim sumere formas; / iamque novum terrae stupeant lucescere solem, / altius atque cadant submotis nubibus imbres; / incipiant silvae cum primum surgere, cumque / rara per ignaros errent animalia montis. / Hinc lapides Pyrrhae iactos, Saturnia regna, / Caucasiasque refert volucres, furtumque Promethei: / his adiungit, Hylan nautae quo fonte relictum / clamassent, ut litus 'Hyla, Hyla!' omne sonaret. / et fortunatam, si numquam armenta fuissent, / Pasiphaen nivei solatur amore iuvenci. / ah, virgo infelix, quae te dementia cepit! / Proetides inplerunt falsis mugitibus agros: / at non tam turpis pecudum tamen ulla secuta est / concubitus, quamvis collo timuisset aratrum, / et saepe in levi quaesisset cornua fronte. / ah, virgo infelix, tu nunc in montibus erras: / ille, latus niveum molli fultus hyacintho, / ilice sub nigra pallentis ruminat herbas, / aut aliquam in magno sequitur grege.

'Claudite, nymphae, / Dictaeae nymphae, nemorum iam claudite saltus, / si qua forte ferant oculis sese obvia nostris / errabunda bovis vestigia; forsitan illum, / aut herba captum viridi, aut armenta secutum, / perducant aliquae stabula ad Gortynia vaccae. / Tum canit Hesperidum miratam mala puellam; / tum Phaethontiades musco circumdat amaro / corticis, atque solo proceras erigit alnos. / Tum canit, errantem Permessi ad flumina Gallum / Aonas in montis ut duxerit una sororum, / utque viro Phoebi chorus adsurrexerit omnis; / ut Linus haec illi, divino carmine pastor, / floribus atque apio crinis ornatus amaro, / dixerit: 'Hos tibi dant calamos, en accipe, Musae, / Ascraeo quos ante seni, quibus ille solebat / cantando rigidas deducere montibus ornos: / his tibi Grynei nemoris dicatur origo, / ne quis sit lucus, quo se plus iactet Apollo.' / Quid loquar aut Scyllam Nisi, quam fama secuta est / candida succinctam latrantibus inguina monstris / Dulichias vexasse rates, et gurgite in alto, / ah, timidos nautas canibus lacerasse marinis, / aut ut mutatos Terei narraverit artus; / quas illi Philomela dapes, quae dona pararit, / quo cursu deserta petiverit, et quibus ante / infelix sua tecta supervolitaverit alis? / Omnia, quae Phoebo quondam meditante, beatus / audiit Eurotas, iussitque ediscere laurus, / ille canit: pulsae referunt ad sidera valles; / cogere donec ovis stabulis numerumque referri / iussit, et invito processit Vesper Olympo.

VII. MELIBOEUS, CORYDON, THYRSIS

M. FORTE sub arguta consederat ilice Daphnis, / compulerantque greges Corydon et Thyrsis in unum, / Trhyrsis ovis, Corydon distentas lacte capellas, / ambo florentes aetatibus, Arcades ambo, / et cantare pares, et respondere parati. / Huc mihi, dum teneras defendo a frigore myrtos, / vir gregis ipse caper deerraverat; atque ego Daphnim / aspicio. Ille ubi me contra videt: 'Ocius' inquit / 'huc ades, O Meliboee, caper tibi salvus et haedi; / et, si quid cessare potes, requiesce sub umbra. / huc ipsi potum venient per prata iuvenci, / hic viridis tenera praetexit arundine ripas / Mincius, eque sacra resonant examina quercu.' / Quid facerem? Neque ego Alcippen, nec Phyllida habebam, / depulsos a lacte domi quae clauderet agnos, / et certamen erat, Corydon cum Thyrside, magnum. / posthabui tamen illorum mea seria ludo: / alternis igitur contendere versibus ambo / coepere; alternos Musae meminisse volebant. / hos Corydon, illos referebat in ordine Thyrsis. / C. Nymphae, noster amor, Libethrides, aut mihi carmen, / quale meo Codro, concedite: proxima Phoebi / versibus ille facit; aut, si non possumus omnes, / hic arguta sacra pendebit fistula pinu. / T. Pastores, hedera crescentem ornate poetam, / Arcades, invidia rumpantur ut ilia Codro; / aut si ultra placitum laudarit, baccare frontem / cingite, ne vati noceat mala lingua futuro. / C. Saetosi caput hoc apri tibi, Delia, parvus / et ramosa Micon vivacis cornua cervi. /

Si proprium hoc fuerit, levi de marmore tota / puniceo stabis suras evincta coturno. / *T.* Sinum lactis et haec te liba, Priape, quotannis / exspectare sat est: custos es pauperis horti. / Nunc te marmoreum pro tempore fecimus; at tu, / si fetura gregem suppleverit, aureus esto. / C. Nerine Galatea, thymo mihi dulcior Hyblae, / candidior cycnis, hedera formosior alba, / cum primum pasti repetent praesepia tauri, / si qua tui Corydonis habet te cura, venito. / *T.* Immo ego Sardoniis videar tibi amarior herbis, / horridior rusco, proiecta vilior alga, / si mihi non haec lux toto iam longior anno est. / Ite domum pasti, si quis pudor, ite iuvenci. / C. Muscosi fontes et somno mollior herba, / et quae vos rara viridis tegit arbutus umbra, / solstitium pecori defendite; iam venit aestas / torrida, iam lento turgent in palmite gemmae. / *T.* Hic focus et taedae pingues, hic plurimus ignis / semper, et adsidua postes fuligine nigri; / hic tantum Boreae curamus frigora, quantum / aut numerum lupus, aut torrentia flumina ripas. / C. Stant et iuniperi, et castaneae hirsutae; / strata iacent passim sua quaque sub arbore poma; / omnia nunc rident: at si formosus Alexis / montibus his abeat, videas et flumina sicca. / *T.* Aret ager; vitio moriens sitit aeris herba; / Liber pampineas invidit collibus umbras: / Phyllidis adventu nostrae nemus omne virebit, / Iuppiter et laeto descendet plurimus imbri. / Populus Alcidae gratissima, vitis Iaccho, / formosae myrtus Veneri, sua laurea Phoebo; / Phyllis amat corylos: illas dum Phyllis amabit, / nec myrtus vincet corylos, nec laurea Phoebi. / *T.* Fraxinus in silvis pulcherrima, pinus in hortis, / populus in fluviis, abies in montibus altis: / saepius at si me, Lycida formose, revisas, / fraxinus in silvis cedat tibi, pinus in hortis. / Haec memini, et victum frustra contendere Thyrsim: / ex illo Corydon Corydon est tempore nobis.

VIII. DAMON, ALPHESIBOEUS

PASTORUM Musam Damonis et Alphesiboei— / immemor herbarum quos est mirata iuvenca / certantis, quorum stupefactae carmine lynces, / et mutata suos requierunt flumina cursus— / Illonis Musam dicemus et Alphesiboei. / Tu mihi seu magni superas iam saxa Timavi, / sive oram Illyrici legis aequoris, en erit umquam / ille dies, mihi cum liceat tua dicere facta? / en erit ut liceat totum mihi ferre per orbem / sola Sophocleo tua carmina digna coturno? / A te principium, tibi desinam: accipe iussis / carmina coepta tuis, atque hanc sine tempora circum / inter victrices hederam tibi serpere laurus. / Frigida vix caelo noctis decesserat umbra, / cum ros in tenera pecori gratissimus herba; / incumbens tereti Damon sic coepit olivae. / *D.* Nascere, praeque diem veniens age, Lucifer, almum, / coniugis indigno Nisae deceptus amore / dum queror, et divos, quamquam nil testibus illis / profeci, extrema moriens tamen adloquor hora. / Incipe Maenalios mecum, mea tibia, versus. / Maenalus argutumque nemus pinosque loquentis / semper habet; semper pastorum ille audit amores, / Panaque, qui primus calaunos non passus inertis. / Incipe Maenalios mecum, mea tibia, versus. / Mopso Nisa datur: quid non speremus amantes? / Iungentur iam grypes equis, aevoque sequenti / cum canibus timidi venient ad pocula dammae. / Mopse, novas incide faces: tibi ducitur uxor; / sparge, marite, nuces: tibi deserit Hesperus Oetam. / Incipe Maenalios mecum, mea tibia, versus. / O digno coniuncta viro, dum despicis omnes, / dumque tibi est odio mea fistula, dumque capellae, / hirsutumque supercilium promissaque barba, / nec curare deum credis mortalia quemquam! / Incipe Maenalios mecum, mea tibia, versus. / Saepibus in nostris parvam te roscida mala— / dux ego vester eram—vidi cum matre legentem. / Alter ab undecimo tum me iam acceperat annus; / iam fragilis poteram ab terra contingere ramos. / Ut vidi, ut perii! Ut me malus abstulit error! / Incipe Maenalios mecum, mea tibia, versus. / Nunc scio, quid sit Amor: duris in cotibus illum / aut Tmaros, aut Rhodope, aut extremm Garamantes, / nec generis nostri puerum nec sanguinis edunt. / Incipe Maenalios mecum, mea tibia, versus. / saevus Amor docuit natorum sanguine matrem / commaculare manus; crudelis tu quoque, mater: / crudelis mater magis, an puer improbus ille? / improbus ille puer; crudelis tu quoque, mater. / Incipe Maenalios mecum, mea tibia, versus. / nunc et ovis ultro fugiat lupus; aurea durae / mala ferant quercus; narcisso floreat alnus; / pinguia corticibus sudent electra myricae; / certent et cycnis ululae; sit Tityrus Orpheus, / Orpheus in silvis, inter delphinas Arion. / Incipe Maenalios mecum, mea tibia, versus. / Omnia vel medium fiant mare: vivite, silvae! / praeceps aerii specula de montis in undas / deferar; extremum hoc munus morientis habeto. / desine Maenalios, iam desine, tibia, versus. / Haec Damon: vos, quae responderit Alphesiboeus, / dicite, Pierides; non omnia possumus omnes. / A. Effer aquam, et molli cinge haec altaria vitta, / verbenasque adole pinguis et mascula tura, / coniugis ut magicis sanos avertere sacris / experiar sensus nihil hic nisi carmina desunt. / Ducite ab urbe domum, mea carmina, ducite Daphnim. / Carmina vel caelo possunt deducere Lunam; / carminibus Circe socios mutavit Ulixi; / frigidus in pratia cantando rumpitur anguis. / Ducite ab urbe domum, mea carmina, ducite Daphnim. / terna tibi haec primum triplici diversa colore / licia circumdo, terque haec altaria circum / effigiem duco: numero deus impare gaudet. / Ducite ab urbe domum, mea carmina, ducite Daphnim. / Necte tribus nodis ternos, Amarylli, colores, / necte, Amarylli, modo, et 'Veneris' dic 'vincula necto.' / Ducite ab urbe domum, mea carmina, ducite Daphnim. / Limus ut hic durescit et haec ut cera liquescit /

uno eodemque igni, sic nostro Daphnis amore. / Sparge molam, et fragilis incende bitumine laurus. / Daphnis me malus urit, ego hanc in Daphnide laurum. / Ducite ab urbe domum, mea carmina, ducite Daphnim. / Talis amor Daphnim, qualis cum fessa iuvencum / per nemora atque altos quaerendo bucula lucos / propter aquae rivum viridi procumbit in ulva, / perdita, nec serae meminit decedere nocti, / talis amor teneat, nec sit mihi cura mederi. / Ducite ab urbe domum, mea carmina, ducite Daphnim. / Has olim exuvias mihi perfidus ille reliquit, / pignora cara sui, quae nunc ego limine in ipso, / terra, tibi mando; debent haec pignora Daphnim. / Ducite ab urbe domum, mea carmina, ducite Daphnim. / Has herbas atque haec Ponto mihi lecta venena / ipse dedit Moeris; nascuntur plurima Ponto. / His ego saepe lupum fieri et se condere silvis / Moerim, saepe animas imis excire sepulcris, / atque satas alio vidi traducere messis. / Ducite ab urbe domum, mea carmina, ducite Daphnim. / Fer cineres, Amarylli, foras, rivoque fluenti / transque caput iace, nec respexeris: his ego Daphnim / adgrediar, nihil ille deos, nil carmina curat. / Ducite ab urbe domum, mea carmina, ducite Daphnim. / Aspice, corripuit tremulis altaria flammis / sponte sua, dum ferre moror, cinis ipse: bonum sit! / Nescio quid certe est, et Hylas in limine latrat. / Credimus, an, qui amant, ipsi sibi somnia fingunt? / Parcite, ab urbe venit, iam carmina, parcite, Daphnis.

IX. LYCIDAS, MOERIS

L. QUO te, Moeri, pedes? an, quo via ducit, in urbem? / *M.* O Lycida, vivi pervenimus, advena nostri / (quod numquam veriti sumus) ut possessor agelli / diceret: 'Haec mea sunt; veteres migrate coloni!' / nunc victi, tristes, quoniam Fors omnia versat, / hos illi—quod nec vertat bene—mittimus haedos. / *L.* Certe equidem audieram, qua se subducere colles / incipiunt, mollique iugum demittere clivo, / usque ad aquam et veteres (iam fracta cacumina) fagos / omnia carminibus vestrum servasse Menalcan. / *M.* Audieras, et fama fuit; sed carmina tantum / nostra valent, Lycida, tela inter Martia, quantum / Chaonias dicunt aquila veniente columbas. / quod nisi me quacumque novas incidere lites / ante Sinistra cava monuisset ab ilice cornix, / nec tuus hic Moeris, nec viveret ipse Menalcas. / *L.* Heu, cadit in quemquam tantum scelus? Heu, tua nobis / paene simul tecum solatia rapta, Menalca? / quis caneret nymphas; quis humum florentibus herbis / spargeret, aut viridi fontes induceret umbra? / vel quae sublegi tacitus tibi carmina nuper, / cum te ad delicias ferres, Amaryllida, nostras? / Tityre, dum redeo—brevis est via—pasce capellas, / et potum pastas age, Tityre, et inter agendum / occursare capro, cornu ferit ille, caveto. / *M.* Immo haec, quae Varo necdum perfecta canebat: / 'Vare, tuum nomen, superet modo Mantua nobis— / Mantua, vae miserae nimium vicina Cremonae— / cantantes sublime ferent ad sidera cycni.' / *L.* Sic tua Cyrneas fugiant examina taxos; / sic cytiso pastae distendant ubera vaccae! / Incipe, si quid habes: et me fecere poetam / Pierides; sunt et mihi carmina; me quoque dicunt / vatem pastores, sed non ego credulus illis. / Nam neque adhuc Vario videor, nec dicere Cinna / digna, sed argutos inter strepere anser olores. / M. Id quidem ago et tacitus, Lycida, mecum ipse voluto, / si valeam meminisse; neque est ignobile carmen: / 'huc ades, O Galatea; quis est nam ludus in undis / hic ver purpureum; varios hic flumina circum / fundit humus flores; hic candida populus antro / imminet, et lentae texunt umbracula vites. / huc ades: insani feriant sine litora fluctus. / *L.* Quid, quae te pura solum sub nocte canentem / audieram? Numeros memini, si verba tenerem. / 'Daphni, quid antiquos signorum suspicis ortus? / Ecce Dionaei processit Caesaris astrum, / astrum, quo segetes gauderent frugibus, et quo / duceret apricis in collibus uva colorem. / insere, Daphni, piros: carpent tua poma nepotes.' / M. Omnia fert aetas, animum quoque: saepe ego longos / cantando puerum memini me condere soles: / nunc oblita mihi tot carmina; vox quoque Moerim / iam fugit ipsa; lupi Moerim videre priores. / Sed tamen ista satis referet tibi saepe Menalcas. / *L.* Causando nostros in longum ducis amores: / et nunc omne tibi stratum silet aequor, et omnes, / aspice, ventosi ceciderunt murmuris aurae. / hinc adeo media est nobis via; namque sepulcrum / incipit adparere Bianoris: hic ubi densas / agricolae stringunt frondes, hic, Moeri, canamus; / hic haedos depone: tamen veniemus in urbem. / aut si, nox pluviam ne colligat ante, veremur, / cantantes licet usque (minus via laedit) eamus; / cantantes ut eamus, ego hoc te fasce levabo. / M. Desine plura, puer, et quod nunc instat agamus: / carmina tum melius, cum venerit ipse, canemus.

X.

EXTREMUM hunc, Arethusa, mihi concede laborem: / pauca meo Gallo, sed quae legat ipsa Lycoris, / carmina sunt dicenda neget quis carmina Gallo? / sic tibi, cum fluctus subterlabere Sicanos, / Doris amara suam non intermisceat undam. / incipe; sollicitos Galli dicamus amores, / dum tenera attondent simae virgulta capellae. / non canimus surdis; respondent omnia silvae. / Quae nemora, aut qui vos saltus habuere, puellae / Naides, indigno cum Gallus amore peribat? / nam neque Parnasi vobis iuga, nam neque Pindi / ulla moram fecere, neque Aoniae Aganippe. / Illum etiam lauri, etiam flevere myricae. / Pinifer illum etiam sola sub rupe iacentem / Maenalus, et gelidi fleverunt saxa Lycaei. / Stant et oves circum;—nostri nec paenitet illas, / nec te poeniteat pecoris, divine poeta;— / et formosus ovis ad flumina pavit Adonis; / venit et upilio; tardi venere subulci; / uvidus hiberna venit de glande Menalcas. / Omnes 'Unde amor iste' rogant 'tibi?' Venit Apollo: / 'Galle, quid insanis?' inquit; 'tua cura Lycoris / perque nives alium perque horrida castra secuta est.' / Venit et agresti capitis Silvanus honore, / florentis ferulas et grandia lilia quassans. / Pan deus Arcadiae venit, quem vidimus ipsi / sanguineis ebuli bacis minioque rubentem. / 'Ecquis erit modus?' inquit; 'Amor non talia curat; / nec lacrimis crudelis Amor, nec gramina rivis, / nec cytiso saturantur apes, nec fronde capellae.' / Tristis at ille: 'Tamen cantabitis, Arcades,' inquit / 'montibus haec vestris: soli cantare periti / Arcades. O mihi tum quam molliter ossa quiescant, / vestra meos olim si fistula dicat amores! / Atque utinam ex vobis unus, vestrique fuissem / aut custos gregis, aut maturae vinitor uvae! / Certe, sive mihi Phillis, sive esset Amyntas, / seu quicumque furor—quid tum, si fuscus Amyntas; / et nigrae violae sunt et vaccinia nigra— / mecum inter salices lenta sub vite iaceret; / serta mihi Phyllis legeret, cantaret Amyntas. / Hic gelidi fontes, hic mollia prata, Lycori, / hic nemus; hic ipso tecum consumerer aevo. / Nunc insanus amor duri me Martis in armis / tela inter media atque adversos detinet hostes: / tu procul a patria (nec sit mihi credere tantum!) / Alpinas, ah dura, nives et frigora Rheni / me sine sola vides: ah, te ne frigora laedant! / ah, tibi ne teneras glacies secet aspera plantas! / Ibo, et, Chalcidico quae sunt mihi condita versu / carmina, pastoris Siculi modulabor avena. / certum est in silvis, inter spelaea ferarum / malle pati, tenerisque meos incidere amores / arboribus; crescent illae, crescetis, amores. / Interea mixtis lustrabo Maenala nymphis, / aut acris venabor apros: non me ulla vetabunt / frigora Parthenios canibus circumdare saltus. / iam mihi per rupes videor lucosque sonantis / ire; libet Partho torquere Cydonia cornu / spicula:—tamquam haec sit nostri medicina furoris, / ut deus ille malis hominum mitescere discat! / Iam neque hamadryades rursus nec carmina nobis / ipsa placent; ipsae rursus concedite silvae. / non illum nostri possunt mutare labores, / nec si frigoribus mediis Hebrumque bibamus, / Sithoniasque nives hiemis subeamus aquosae, / nec si, cum moriens alta liber aret in ulmo, / Aethiopum versemus ovis sub sidere Cancri. / omnia vincit Amor; et nos cedamus Amori.' / Haec sat erit, divae, vestrum cecinisse poetam, / dum sedet et gracili fiscellam texit hibisco, / Pierides; vos haec facietis maxima Gallo— / Gallo, cuius amor tantum mihi crescit in horas, / quantum vere novo viridis se subicit alnus. / Surgamus; solet esse gravis cantantibus umbra; / iuniperi gravis umbra; nocent et frugibus umbrae. / te domum saturae, venit Hesperus, ite capellae.

www.ingramcontent.com/pod-product-compliance
Ingram Content Group UK Ltd.
Pitfield, Milton Keynes, MK11 3LW, UK
UKHW020427250726
13967UKWH00007B/2837

9 780244 034771